PRAVE

PRAVE

The Adventures of the Blind and the Brittle

DAVE BAHR

BOW STRING PRESS

Prave: The Adventures of the Blind and the Brittle
Published by BOWSTRING PRESS
Louisville, Colorado

Library of Congress Control Number: 2019900213
ISBN: 978-0-692-14954-6

BIOGRAPHY & AUTOBIOGRAPHY / People with Disabilities
BODY, MIND & SPIRIT / Inspiration & Personal Growth

Cover Design by Nick Zelinger
Interior Design by Andrea Costantine
Editing by Catherine Spader

QUANTITY PURCHASES: Schools, companies, professional
groups, clubs, and other organizations may qualify for special
terms when ordering quantities of this title. For information, email
BOWSTRING PRESS at Info@BowstringPress.com

For Priscilla Darlene Carlson: With a love that will always transcend language, time, and space.

Priscilla's engagement ring surrounded by leaves

CONTENTS

Introduction

This is a story about two people with different disabilities. A lot of these types of books exist in bookstores and online. I'm sure some of them are fantastic, and others should be discarded. Hopefully, what you are presently holding is the former and not the latter—not least because you might be listening to it on an audio device or reading it on an expensive e-book reader or your smart phone, and I would hate for you to get rid of those on my account. But I digress.

This book is about two people with different disabilities who complemented each other. These two people didn't set out to be anybody's inspiration but were merely trying to live their lives. You can probably guess that I am one of the two. I'm Dave, and my wife was Priscilla. This is our story. My goal in writing this book is not only for you to cherish Priscilla, as I did, but to learn more about the misunderstandings of disability, as well as learn more about self-advocacy, being human, and love.

My disability is total blindness from birth. Priscilla had *osteogenesis imperfecta* (also known as brittle bones). We grew up in very different settings, with very different parents, and in different generations. Priscilla was nine years older than I was, but we knew our respective domains and how to deal with life on our own terms. We came together in a cataclysmic force of advocacy, romance, and love, and realized what a great team we would make.

This is a story about two people who overcame each other's shortcomings by becoming the other's "other half," and had one hell of a time doing it.

As you can probably tell from the way I've written this, Priscilla has passed away. It happened on May 25, 2017, and the cause was a brain aneurysm. I promise you, though, by the end of this story, you will understand why this was a blessing in the end. I can also promise you that along the way, there will be moments of raucous laughter, fear, joy, sadness, and incredulity at the behavior of other people we interacted with. There might also be moments of disgust, hopefully not at our behavior, although we cannot claim to be perfectly sentient beings.

If you are able to see the cover image of Priscilla and me in our wedding attire, you probably thought, "That's a cute couple. Kind of strange looking. I wonder what that's about." That's what I would've thought upon seeing that image. "How did these two find each other—a blind man and a small woman in a wheelchair?" Read our story and you'll see our life was a roller coaster, just like any couple's experience. But there were more hills on this coaster than on your average amusement park thrill ride. We went from college students in love to a married couple who held down jobs and paid a mortgage, and we survived and thrived in the face of arrogance, chosen ignorance, and plain misunderstanding of what being disabled means.

But, before we get started, let's talk candidly about disability and political correctness. To me, being politically correct is offensive. Political correctness was made up by somebody who doesn't have a disability, and so they coined terms like "differently abled." I'm not a big fan of the word disability, but I use it because it's the word that people understand. I think something as inane as "differently abled" is condescending. The difference between political correctness and someone being offensive is that they are trying to be sensitive when being politically correct. They are trying to be empathetic to someone else's differences—differences that they themselves will never understand unless they share them. Just as you, the reader, would not know what it's like to be blind (unless, of course, you are and you're reading this), I will never know what it's like to live in a tribe in Africa where I send my children to school, and they could possibly get eaten by lions!

I understand you have no idea what it's like to be me. This book is intended to show you things that you never knew, just like I never knew what it was like to be Priscilla when she broke a bone or had a kidney stone. However, we shared empathy for each other. In fact, we talked about that one day.

Priscilla said, "The first thing I do in the morning is see. I look for my glasses or the remote to turn on the light switch."

I responded, "And the first thing I do is reach over to find the smooth surface of my phone's screen to turn off the alarm." They were both actions we took, and took for granted, that the other couldn't do.

I understand that people don't want to offend, but rather than saying you don't want to offend me (which immediately puts me on the defensive, ready to take a punch), ask how I'd like to be treated. Ignorance is simply not knowing, but if you are open to overcoming that ignorance, that is what this book is aiming to help you do. That's what Priscilla and I spent our lives doing—educating people about disability, whether at the airport, a restaurant, or in the entire home care industry.

This book includes stories of people who were offensive and stories of people who were compassionate and understanding. At times, people were offensive and had no clue of it. Some of them we told outright, but some of them just needed to be taught a lesson in a subtler way. The important thing is that Priscilla and I were advocates for what we believed in. I want to share that story of advocacy with you. The best thing that anybody who does not understand another person's view can do is to empathize and be open to learning new and interesting things.

CHAPTER ONE

Beginnings:
Blue Babies and Broken Bones

Remember when you were in middle school, and you had to write a biography or research paper on someone? Well, I had an instructor who said simply, "You have to find out about the person, you can't just say, 'He was born, he lived, and he died.'"

I was born November 16, 1986, with a twin brother whose name is Matt. My sister, Suriah, was watching angrily from outside the nursery window at the two new creatures that were invading her two-year-old world. My brother and I were born three months prematurely at twenty-six weeks' gestation and were not expected to survive. Our lungs and hearts were not fully developed, so we had patches of blue on our skin due to a lack of circulation, and Matt was purple except for a spot on his leg. The nurses thought, somehow, that we were only twenty-four weeks, even with my parents' insistence that we were twenty-six. It was a close call, but somehow, we made it despite being born in Lubbock, Texas, where technology wasn't exactly up to snuff.

As a preemie, I was affected by retinopathy of prematurity, in which the retinas detach from the eyes, causing blindness. It occurs most often in premature babies. Receiving too much oxygen after birth increases the risk of the condition.

By the time the delivery staff figured out what was happening, my left retina had already detached. The retina in my right eye, however, had not separated. Unfortunately, time was of the essence. My eye got mixed signals from my brain, and the fibers that were supposed to be growing as nerve fibers were growing as muscle fibers instead. This resulted in the ripping of the retina from the back of my right eye. Being only six months old at the time, I don't remember any of it.

My dad, Chuck, took me around the country to different clinics to see what they could do. We ended up in Houston, where a doctor performed surgery that destroyed the eye, so my right eye is a prosthetic. My left eye became a mess of scar tissue after it was subjected to, what was then, the forefront of laser surgery in 1987 by a doctor in Memphis. Other than a tiny bit of light perception in my left eye, I have been blind ever since.

In 1989, my family moved from Midland, Texas, to Denver, Colorado. My dad was a petroleum geologist working for Texaco at the time. He had sent a letter to the corporate offices, asking to be transferred to Denver because he had a blind son, and the school districts in Denver were better than the ones in Houston where they might have transferred his department. The letter went up the chain of command, and the request was granted. I grew up in Colorado and barely remember anything Texan, aside from the fact that country music is in my blood—at least that's what I blame it on.

I attribute the start of my education to a wonderful organization, the Anchor Center for Blind Children in Denver. This is a preschool designed for blind and low-vision children. That's where I began learning braille, a system of raised dots that can be read with the fingers. It was invented in France in the nineteenth century by Louis Braille, and a lot of blind people use it to read. I was so good at reading braille that by the time I left preschool, I had learned four letters. Rarely had such a feat ever been achieved (insert sarcasm here). But it was a start.

To this day, I am still very good friends with one of the original founders of Anchor Center. I find it to be an extremely worthy cause, so I have done numerous speaking engagements there, talking to parents who were just as frightened as mine were, and sharing my story of advocacy.

My parents were often asked whether I would also attend the School for the Deaf and Blind located in Colorado Springs. They asked teachers about it when I was in elementary school, and the answer was always the same: No. I later learned my parents chose to keep me in a school district with better educational standards than the School for the Deaf and Blind offered at that time, and for that, I'm thankful.

Instead, I received my education from an affluent school district in Colorado. I was just like every other kid, except I couldn't see. I experienced everything that other kids experience in elementary, middle school, and high school, except I didn't like recess because I could not keep up with kids running on the playground. During my one attempt at basketball, I asked if I could throw the ball. The play was stopped, and the other kids didn't know what to do because the blind kid wanted to throw a basketball at a hoop that he couldn't see. The end result was not successful.

After high school, I went to the University of Denver for two years before transferring to the University of Colorado at Boulder to finish my bachelor's in psychology with an emphasis in music. I then earned a master's degree in musicology. I had played the piano from age four to age ten, and the fiddle throughout middle school and high school. Despite being horrible at fiddle, in eighth grade, I was able to go with the school orchestra to California to play at Disneyland. I also attended the Rocky Mountain Fiddle Camp before my junior year of high school. It was a lot of fun. I was even taught the proper way to hold a violin bow, which, apparently, my previous fiddle instructor had decided not to teach me.

Camp included some great players, and I still have pictures of me with all of them. In college, I took voice lessons to get into the college of music. I did private study and joined a couple of choirs, and even auditioned for a cappella groups. But my real love of music was not in playing it but in researching it. This is where my desire to earn a musicology degree came in. We'll hear more about that when Priscilla and I meet up shortly. Speaking of Priscilla, let's fill you in on where she stands, or sits, in this whole story.

Priscilla was born on February 20, 1978, in the small town of Grafton, North Dakota. She was a full-term baby and weighed about eight pounds. She had so much hair, her parents had to put it in a bun on the top of her head. True to form, Priscilla was late, a trend that would continue practically unabated for the rest of her life.

There was just one problem. She had nine broken bones at the time of her delivery. In 1978 in a small town, these were bad signs that could only be explained by horrible traumatic events. She was immediately taken away to Grand Forks, and neither her mother, Darlene, nor her father, Cledith, was allowed to hold her, and they only saw her briefly. Her parents were detained and questioned by social services, which also became a trend throughout Priscilla's childhood. Social services asked Darlene if she had been in a car accident or if her husband beat her. Shocked, she had simply answered, "No!"

Darlene was told that her daughter had nine broken bones and three more had broken on the way to the hospital in Grand Forks. Nobody could figure out what was wrong because Priscilla would not cry when she was in the bassinet, but when somebody picked her up, she would howl in pain. Everybody was puzzled.

Coincidentally, a medical conference was in town at the time, and some of the leading orthopedic doctors were attending. A doctor from Germany examined Priscilla and diagnosed what she had: osteogenesis imperfecta (OI), more commonly referred to as brittle bones. The doctor said he could tell by the whites of her eyes, which had a bluish tint—a characteristic of OI.

OI is congenital and genetic. It was also something that a typical family of four in Park River, North Dakota (population 1,400 or so), had never heard of and didn't know what to do with. This condition didn't present itself in Priscilla's older brother, Dion, who arrived nine years earlier in perfect health.

Once the diagnosis had been made, the family was able to see their daughter. They received some (insert sarcasm here) helpful and sound advice for moving forward that sounded something like, "Okay, we know what she has. It's called osteogenesis imperfecta or brittle bones. So, just take care of her and do whatever you can to make sure that she doesn't break a bone. Got it? Okay, here you go."

See what I mean by helpful? Yeah, didn't think so. So, that's what they tried to do as best as they could for the next thirty-nine years: stop her from breaking any bones. The doctors actually didn't know what to do before Priscilla was about five. They kept purposefully breaking her bones and casting them to try and get them to grow straighter. Keep in mind, this was 1980 in rural North Dakota.

People with OI have strange things happen with their bones in childhood; they rarely grow straight bones. Around age four or five, Priscilla's family was introduced to the Shriners Hospital for Crippled Children in Minneapolis (yes, that was the full name of it back then). Not only did they provide free medical care, but they also were interested in doing an experimental surgery that included placing rods into Priscilla's arms and legs. The steel rods were designed to telescope like a radio antenna as she grew. At that point, Priscilla's bones bowed so much, she was sitting on her feet and her legs were under her. Priscilla's parents asked her if she wanted to do the surgery. They always wanted the decision to be hers because she was such an articulate child. That's not to say they weren't scared, and they hated to leave her behind at the hospital because they had to work, and their son Dion was back home in Park River.

This choice saved Priscilla's life. In fact, another family with a little boy who had OI opted not to do the surgery because of its experimental nature. The result, as Priscilla saw some years later, was extremely sad to witness. He could not sit up, could not scratch his right wrist with his left hand, and always had to have an assistant with him. After the surgeries had been completed, Priscilla's bones grew straighter. Although they still cracked and broke, the rods held them in place. Priscilla's friend Teresa was ten years younger and had titanium rods in her bones. Priscilla always said, "I'm the T100 and Teresa is the T1000" in reference to the *Terminator* movies.

At one point, Priscilla was told by the therapists at Shriners Hospital that she had to start walking. Nowadays we would probably think this was ludicrous, but at the time you weren't "normal" unless you were walking. This really made no sense because Priscilla was so short, and nobody would see her even if she could walk, creating even more of a safety risk for her. Nonetheless, they strapped her to a board and put braces on her and tried to get her to walk. The pain was excruciating.

After some time, a boil formed on the right side of her right leg. The doctor she saw to treat it practiced in a small North Dakota town. He lied, convincing Priscilla that he was not going to touch it and that she should turn over. Without telling her, he lanced it! It contained so much pressure that whatever was inside shot out and hit the opposite wall, and Priscilla screamed. That was a horrible thing to do—to lie to a kid. Then it got worse. That same doctor began to treat the area by burning it with silver nitrate. The pain and the smell were both nauseating.

After several treatments of the silver nitrate had not fixed the problem, Darlene called the Shriners Hospital in Minneapolis, and they instructed her to bring Priscilla in immediately. The doctors at Shriners were appalled at the use of such primitive medicinal techniques. Unfortunately, Darlene and Cledith had not known any better because that doctor had been a trusted, local professional.

Priscilla developed a staph infection from the boil-lancing treatment, and she had to be put in isolation. So, to recap, the braces she was forced to wear to make her walk caused a boil, and the boil treatment led to a staph infection. This infection required her to have her rods removed in order to clear the infection. Once clear, they were replaced. This entire process took about five months. Priscilla was only six years old at the time. This also resulted in her right leg not growing as long as her left, leaving it about an inch shorter. To add insult to injury, the folks at Shriners apparently hadn't learned their lesson. The infection had cleared, and Priscilla had recovered enough, so they said, "Okay Priscilla, time to start walking again."

Priscilla replied, in what I'm sure was an agonized, pitiful voice, "But I don't want to walk, it hurts." She threw a fit, as any kid would do in this situation. She demanded to talk to her mom. The hospital staff relented, and Priscilla was able to call collect (remember those days?) to her mom.

She said, "Mom, they want me to walk again."

Darlene asked simply, "Well, do you want to walk again?"

Priscilla, through tears, replied, "No, it hurts!"

"Put 'em on the phone," said Darlene.

The way Priscilla told the story summed up Darlene's tirade. "Yeah, Mom basically ripped them a new one by saying, 'If Priscilla doesn't want to walk, she's not going to walk. Look at how short she is! She'd get stepped on, and look at all she's just been through!'" Needless to say, Priscilla never did walk after that.

Both Priscilla and I had to grow up fast and learn how to advocate for ourselves before the term "self-advocacy" existed. It bonded and connected us. Despite all the medical issues and pain, there was a person behind the small stature and seemingly countless surgeries— a very intelligent, talkative, and positive person named Priscilla.

Chapter Two

Canes and Curb Cuts

My independence started at about age four when I began to learn how to use a cane (just for the record, it is not called a "stick, staff, or pole"). At that time and for the next several years, I had an orientation and mobility instructor show me how to cross streets and take buses.

While Priscilla was in my life, I didn't pay as much attention to my mobility needs because she guided me everywhere. Before that, I would meet with somebody at the beginning of every school year and have them help me navigate to my classes. Sometimes this was an orientation and mobility instructor, but later, in college, it was a disabilities services advisor.

For me, gaining independence involved mentors who were also blind, such as the piano teacher I had when I was four. Gail was totally blind and went everywhere with her guide dog. She inspired my father to push me to also be independent.

Another mentor whom I had the pleasure of meeting when I was about sixteen was the actor and writer Tom Sullivan. He was most famous for the book and movie, *If You Could See What I Hear*. Doctors told his parents in the late 1940s, "Oh, Mr. Sullivan, your son is blind; you should institutionalize him."

When Tom Sullivan told me this, my jaw dropped. That was the medical thinking of the times, and had been for centuries. People who were blind were either beggars, piano tuners, or locked up just because they couldn't see.

Achieving my independence was not just limited to physical movement, but also involved advocacy to get what I needed. I had an aide named Sue for eleven years as a child. She became (and still is) like a second mother to me.

In the third grade, I remember Sue saying, "Okay, it's time for you to order your own books now."

As I grew up, my responsibility for my education slowly evolved from that. Sue's role changed from helping me organize things to being my braille transcriber and typing up papers that I needed in hard copy. In my senior year, she had to resign her position and take a full-time elementary school teaching job. At that point, it was up to me to get most of the materials to the district braille transcriber.

I didn't want to do that but was told that I had to, or I wouldn't get my books for the year. So, reluctantly, I called the Utah State Library, which houses many braille volumes, and ordered what I needed. This opened the door to easily using the telephone, which proved very useful when I wanted to call places like Best Buy or Walmart to see if they had a particular CD or video game. I still have no problem picking up a phone and calling for things I need.

As I got older, it became automatic to call and order my books myself. I heard through the grapevine that other students my age were still having their aides or vision itinerant teachers call in their books, even in high school. (A vision itinerant teaches braille and helps students in the classroom. I was lucky because I had an aide and a vision itinerant teacher.)

This early experience with independence put me ahead of the game. When I went to college, what I had learned about self-advocacy and independence in high school paid off in spades. I knew how to schedule my own classes, get things scanned into electronic format, and I was pretty good at navigating with a cane. But something was missing.

In 2005, I was awarded a college scholarship from the American Council of the Blind. They flew me to Las Vegas to accept the award. It was my first time flying without a family member. I met some people whom I still call my friends (one of them ended up being a groomsman in my wedding), but I also noticed a bunch of people who were blind and accompanied by dogs. I asked one of them to guide me around, not knowing that a guide dog doesn't like that sort of thing. A dog is trained to work with only one person, so it got confused when I held onto the person's elbow. Why should the dog have to guide two people? Despite this, I was impressed at how well they got around with their dogs.

When I went back home, I didn't tell anybody, but I had a new appreciation for the guide dog. Earlier in life, I had vowed to never get one—I didn't feel I needed one and didn't want the responsibility. I had said I'd never get one. Never say never.

Around the middle of October at the University of Denver, I was walking down a path I had walked many times before in order to get to class. I recall vividly standing in the middle of that path, picturing myself holding a dog harness. It was like some sort of apparition that appeared before me. I stopped walking and stood there for a second. I usually don't believe in signs, but this was a sign. It was time for me to get a dog.

I had an interview with Guiding Eyes for the Blind

in February 2006. They accepted me into the program, and I found out they would have a dog available to me around the end of March. On July 26, I flew to Yorktown Heights, New York, just having returned from a European cruise two days earlier. In New York, I completed a twenty-six-day program to learn how to take care of a dog and how to work with her. It was very intensive with full, twelve-hour days. It cost a total of $40,000 for the training, all financed through fundraising. The majority of dogs don't make it to guide dog status because of the rigorous training—they just don't have the temperament.

I learned the basics of pet care, such as walking and feeding, because I hadn't done that previously. "Working with the dog" means learning harnessing, behaviors, correction, communication, and how it guides you. You also learn to work as a team with your dog. It can take up to a year to bond and understand each other.

My parents had a very small Yorkshire terrier, so when Katie, a black Labrador, came wandering in with one of the trainers, she seemed like a big dog to me. She had just turned two years old and was full of attitude and the insatiable hunger for, well, food! Those twenty-six days of training were some of the most stressful, exhilarating, and ultimately rewarding ones of my life. It took Katie and me seven months to really click. During that time, she and I worked together constantly, and I had feedback from others on how to handle her. She would remain my guide dog for the next ten years. I am now an independent traveler, thanks to Katie and all of my mobility instructors.

Let's turn now to Priscilla and look at her path toward independence.

Remember how I told you that the doctors gave Priscilla to her parents and simply said, "Be careful and make sure she doesn't break a bone"? That is what Cledith and Darlene did, trying the best they could for the first twenty-nine years of Priscilla's life. Despite their efforts, she broke and cracked bones. Social services came in a few times to check on possible abuse causing the fractures, which was unfounded. Her parents were doing the best they could without any guidance.

Priscilla was homeschooled until the Americans with Disabilities Act (ADA) was passed in 1990. At that time, she was told she could go to public school, but she replied, "I don't want to go to public school. I don't know anybody!"

In a town of fourteen hundred, she was sure to get noticed, and she did. She attended seventh through twelfth grade as an outcast because she was different. The feeling of being an outcast became another thing that bonded us when we met. However, her intelligence, sense of humor, exceedingly outspoken personality, and charm made her a force to be reckoned with in every way possible.

After high school, she worked at a telemarketing agency and a customer service agency, then became a supervisor, and eventually became the assistant site supervisor. She was responsible for conducting trainings and writing parts of the company manual. It took her twelve years to move from being a starting-wage phone representative to obtaining a managerial position within the company.

In 2000, Priscilla went to a conference for the OI Foundation in Milwaukee, Wisconsin. It was close to North Dakota, so she and her family could drive. While there, she met a woman named Lisa who also had OI and drove a manual wheelchair. She was bigger than Priscilla, and a little older. Priscilla always called herself "the runt," because she was the smallest of all the people she knew with OI, with her "T. rex (short) arms."

Lisa was doing a lot of things that Priscilla couldn't do. She drove a car, had a service dog named Gismo, and was studying to become an engineer at the Colorado School of Mines in Golden, Colorado. Priscilla could not place where she had seen Lisa before, but she knew she had seen her somewhere. If there was one thing Priscilla knew well, it was TV, because she watched a ton of it growing up. It turned out that Lisa had been on an episode of the children's show *Reading Rainbow* when she was a teenager. This was around 1990 or so. Small world, eh?

Priscilla's parents were so afraid that she would break a bone that they did everything for her, from helping her get dressed, to salting her food, to helping her in and out of bed. They did it all.

Lisa and Priscilla spent the next seven years emailing nearly every day. Priscilla, meanwhile, was working at a call center as assistant supervisor, and really not liking it. She had started out as a telemarketer after graduating high school. As she said, "I needed to work. What else could someone do in a wheelchair in the mid'90s but be on the phone?" Priscilla's job was stressful and depressing. She drank, a lot, and she once said, "I spent my twenties in a bar. There's not much to do in North Dakota except drink and pop out babies. Well, I wasn't going to do the last one, but I could drink full-grown men under the table." She was also having moral conflicts with selling people things that they didn't need and training other people to do the same. Something had to change.

In 2007, Lisa asked Priscilla to be in her wedding, so Priscilla and her father traveled to Colorado in March. She took a leave of absence from work to help Lisa plan her wedding, as well. Priscilla planned the bridal shower and bachelorette party and noticed how different

Colorado was than North Dakota. In Park River, North Dakota, the streets had curb cuts (what people often call the wheelchair ramps) on only one side of the street. In Colorado, they had curb cuts on both sides, and they had wheelchair-accessible buses. Because of the ease of mobility, Lisa went everywhere. She even had a car and was getting dressed on her own. This was exciting and raised the question in Priscilla's mind, "Why can't I do that?"

CHAPTER THREE

Lust in the Lab

I met Priscilla Carlson in the spring of 2010. It was the second semester of my graduate program. One of my Disabilities Services advisors told me there would be a meeting of people who were interested in advocacy and going to the meeting would be a good way for me to socialize and meet other people. I was quite antisocial, generally depressed, and not in good shape physically. So, after much grumbling and muttering about being with other people of my "own kind," Katie and I went to the meeting.

The person who was running the meeting was in a manual wheelchair, was an intern, and seemed nice enough. The meeting was about self-advocacy and the creation of some sort of organization where people could have a voice in the community. At the time, I didn't give a shit about the community, and I couldn't care less about having a voice. Remember, antisocial here, and suffering from depression—and I looked like hell. I already felt like I understood self-advocacy and didn't know why I needed to go back to things I'd known how to do since I was twelve. It pissed me off to be there.

Eventually, the question was raised as to what we would call this stupid, fucking organization. I was already annoyed because I didn't want to have anything more to do with self-advocacy. I had done enough of that just trying to get to school, and I didn't feel like passing on my oh-so-wise ways to others of the same species. My bitterness only mounted as people threw out names. And then, the leader said, "What do you think, Priscilla?"

In that moment, I heard a voice unlike anything I had ever heard before or will ever hear again. It was strange. It wasn't squeaky; it sounded like a child, but an extremely articulate, happy, bold child. I don't remember what she said; it was simply her voice that had an impact on me. I do remember that somebody came up with a name for the group: the Council for Inclusion, Leadership, and Advocacy. Also known as CILA.

I looked away, the scowl prominent on my lips. Fuck this. Why the fuck do I want to be included? I stared off into space as people talked around me. I looked horrible. I had been struggling with painkiller addiction on and off for the past few years. I was emaciated, I hadn't shaved in a few days, and I probably smelled bad, to boot. At this moment, I'm sure you could sense the romance blossoming in the air.

As the meeting finally, and thankfully, came to a close, I heard a noise behind me. I was about to get up and leave when that articulate, happy, bold voice spoke to me.

"Hi! I'm Priscilla! What's your name?"

"Dave." I was in no mood to talk.

She kept on, "Oh, you have a beautiful dog, what's his name?"

"Her name's Katie." Really? I stared down, it wasn't like I could look her in the eye anyway.

The silence stretched a few more seconds. Then she said rather awkwardly, "Well, have a good day."

"Yeah, uh, you too." I didn't even hear the sound of her wheelchair as I got my things and left. Much later, I asked her what she thought of that first meeting. The response was vintage Priscilla Carlson, "I thought you were a dick. You looked horrible, and you looked like you didn't want to be there. But your dog was cute."

The first impression is always the most memorable. I remembered her name and her distinctive voice. I also remember thinking over the next year or so, "Priscilla, a unique name and voice, but how the hell was I going to find her when I didn't know what she looked like?"

This was the story of my fucking dating life. Dave meets girl, likes girl, wants to find girl again, but if girl makes no noise, then Dave will never find girl. And, yes, that's happened before.

Fast-forward a full year later to March 2011. I was now halfway through my second year as a musicology master student at the University of Colorado, Boulder. I was working in the Assistive Technology Lab almost every other day. I had recently received a new braille display. This is a machine that shows me electronic, refreshable braille. Think of it as a blind person's equivalent of a monitor, just a lot more expensive. Anyway, the display had some sort of issue with it. One of the dots in one of the cells, like a pixel in the bottom left-hand corner of a computer screen, wasn't working right. To a sighted person, a pixel is just an eyesore of an annoyance that you are drawn to instinctively, but a dot missing on a braille display changes the entire meaning of a word or letter. There are only sixty-four combinations of six dots in braille. It would be like leaving all of the tails off of printed letters—they just wouldn't make sense. You might as well be speaking Japanese (no offense to the Japanese out there). This braille display was supposed to be new and had cost around $6,200. A dot not working was infuriating.

So, naturally, as one might suspect in a technology lab, I was complaining about technology, or rather, about the shipping of my technology to the manufacturer. I was talking to myself, bitching out loud, when I heard a familiar voice say, "Wait, what?! They can't do that! Who are these people? You want me to talk to 'em?"

I knew that distinct, unforgettable voice. "Oh, hi Dave, it's Priscilla. That's bullshit! They can't expect you to pay shipping both ways, especially considering … wait how much was that thing you got there?"

"Uh, well, um … a lot. Like $6,200." I didn't know her from Adam, but rarely had I heard such anger well up so quickly. I turned around to face her. She was sitting at the printer table that moved up and down for people in wheelchairs.

"Seriously, that's not right. You want me to talk to them? 'Cause I will! Shipping both ways, please. Huh …"

"Um, well," I sighed, "I kinda just want it fixed, and if that's what I have to do …"

"NO! You won't pay shipping both ways, and if I have to find out who they are myself, I will do just that." She said it with a venom. I would come to love seeing her venom fly from her pretty lips and flushed face. This chick meant business.

"Uh, well, I just want it fixed, really. I'll talk to them.

Maybe I didn't read something right, which would make sense considering this shit is broken."

A good friend of mine took me to The UPS Store that evening, and I didn't really think about meeting Priscilla that day. I just wanted to get that thing fixed. It wasn't until I came in a day or so later and she was sitting by herself at that same desk (her habitual spot), that things began to change.

I don't remember which conversation came first, but I do know we had both of these exchanges in a short period of time. Walking by her desk, I think I might have tripped or nearly tripped over the back of her wheelchair. I don't know what made me say it, but I said, just without really thinking, "You know, I dated a girl in a wheelchair in high school."

It was true. That girl had been my first serious relationship. Priscilla's response, however, told me that a serious relationship was unlikely to happen after that statement.

"Oh yeah?! How'd that go for you?!" Her snarky retort left me stammering.

I started spluttering, "Well, um, I mean, it was fine, she …" I was just trying to make conversation. Later, Priscilla told me her perspective about that moment:

"The look on your face was so sad and hurt. You looked like somebody had just slapped you, and I thought to myself, 'Priscilla, you are a fucking bitch! He's just awkward and it's not his fault that you're bitter and there are creepers out there.'"

She had thought I was feeding her a pickup line. I was doing nothing of the kind. I was just trying to make conversation relating to something I knew a little about. Granted, the girl I had dated was full-sized and was in a manual chair, but, I mean, a wheelchair was at least the common denominator—or so I thought. What I did not know until much later was that she thought I was going to be like some people she (and others in chairs) had encountered online. These were men who had, for lack of a better term, a wheelchair fetish. Or they at least wanted to "take care" of the woman in question. As Priscilla said, "It was creepy. I'd get messages that just said, 'Wow, you're pretty. I'd take care of you, you know.'"

Right?! That's fucked up. It's the idea that the men wanted to have power over the woman. And in Priscilla's case, she had no defense, so this kind of proposition was a roundabout way of being dominant. When I took care of her, it was in a far more conventional and egalitarian manner. She wanted to be more than objectified.

Then came the conversation that has become infamous, so much so that we asked our officiant to recite it at our wedding. It happened in the assistive technology lab. I was talking about something or other, and the conversation went silent for a moment. Then Priscilla asked, "So, what are you studying?"

She asked as if I was in prison and had just committed some sort of crime worthy of scorn.

"A master's in musicology."

Her response was deadpan, "Oh yeah? What are you going to do with that?"

I gave the standard response which I had used before with a few other people: "Probably live under a bridge clutching my master's thesis."

She laughed, but it wasn't just a small laugh, it was a full-throated one that shook her violently. I smiled. Score! I had cracked the exterior shell of Priscilla Carlson. But if she could dish it out, there was no sense in me mincing words either, so I fired back, "How about you? What are you here for?"

"I'm getting a double major in broadcast news and political science."

I wasn't quite sure what to make of this, but I went with it, seeing as the scales were tipped in my direction, and they had to be balanced out. "And what are you going to do with that?"

I tried to mimic her deadpan delivery as much as possible. There was a pause, then she said, as if thinking aloud, "Probably live under that same bridge filming the poor shmuck clutching his dissertation and hoping to make a break on YouTube or something."

Now, it was my turn to laugh wholeheartedly with a broad grin on my face. I hadn't laughed like that in a long time. I thought to myself, "Hmmm, I like her, should I … ah what the fuck, why not, what have I got to lose?"

I said it without really putting the words together in my head before they came out of my mouth, but this time they landed on a far better target than those of my previous blunder. "Hey, you're pretty cool, want to go for a beer?"

She said yes, and we exchanged contact information. I arrived back at my computer to find an email requesting a date and time.

CHAPTER FOUR

Music, Beer, and Boba

I remember exactly what we ate on our first date because of the significance it had later. To tell you the truth, everything had some sort of significance on this date. I had a pizza, but I know that Priscilla had chicken strips. When I asked her later about that, she said, "You can't go wrong with chicken strips. It's something I probably wouldn't spill on myself, which I'm very good at doing."

This was true. She and her father had contests to see who would spill on their shirt first. Priscilla usually won. The ironic part was that I couldn't see whether she had spilled or not. I think she thought about that later on.

After we placed our orders, we continued our

conversation. Priscilla said, "Now the waiter is looking at both of us as if he's shocked that we are actually alive and carrying on a conversation."

This was a look that we often experienced throughout the next six years. I admit, we made a striking couple (trio if you count the dog). Priscilla said people looked at us as if we had fallen from the sky. This is an example of when somebody does not know that they are being offensive, but they also don't know what to do with a situation that they have never encountered before. In this case, the waiter felt uncomfortable knowing that I couldn't see. This happens all the time. He had two choices: either look at me or look away from me. He chose the second choice, which was inadvertently offensive. It's happened so many times in my life that I really don't get too peeved about it. I also can tell where somebody is by the sound of the person's voice. I knew that he was looking away, but I just wanted the date to continue, so it was really a triviality. He should have looked at me straight on and talked toward my face, despite the fact that I was wearing dark glasses. For the record, the ultimate sin by a restaurant service person is to ask the person at the table who is sighted what I would like to order. If my father is asked for my menu choice, he will most likely say something to the effect of, "I don't know, ask him!" It always makes me laugh.

My and Priscilla's chemistry and conversations were almost instantaneous. I didn't feel nervous around her, probably because I wasn't doing a lot of the talking. Little did I know I was being set up, and the game of twenty questions was about to begin. Men are so thick sometimes.

So are people, especially when they see a dog. When the harness is on, the dog is working. For me, that's the rule, because I know that I get distracted easily, and so does Katie. I bring this up now because while our conversations flowed easily, Priscilla and I were constantly interrupted by people wanting to pet my dog.

Between interruptions, Priscilla asked, "So did you like Obama's State of the Union?"

"Oh yeah, I love him! He really knows how to work the crowd and get his point across, although I could do without all of the clapping for every little thing he says."

I later realized that Priscilla was subtly asking if I was a Democrat. Okay, she could check that one off the list. I also found out her last date had been a Republican who was less than enthusiastic about the current Obama administration. This was not going to fly with Priscilla Carlson, the news-reporting, policy-driven, North Dakota transplant. Needless to say, my response was definitely more up her alley.

Then it was my turn to ask a question. "So, what about music? I study classical music and listen to a lot of jazz."

Here we go, I thought, this is when I find out that she listens to the most annoying pop music possible and considers jazz to be a lesser form of art, if it is art at all.

Her response floored me and still does to this day. "I'm not like your typical girl listening to all that poppy shit. I like older music like Sam Cooke, the Everly Brothers, Elvis, the Beatles, music like that. I also love older movies with people like Katharine Hepburn and Cary Grant."

I thought my dreams had come true! Somebody about my age actually knew who Sam Cooke was! Sam Cooke was my singing idol, along with Tim Buckley and Van Morrison. I knew nearly everything Cooke had done and had it easily accessible on my computer. I nearly choked on my beer.

"You know who Sam Cooke is?" I imagine the look on her face was like the one the waiter had given us—as if I had dropped down from outer space.

"Yeah, my mom loves him, and Elvis," she said. "I'm named after Elvis's wife, Priscilla. My brother is eight years older than me, and his name is Dion after Dion and the Belmonts. My mom wanted to name him Elvis, but my dad said that he would divorce her if she did that."

The world, including the slice of pizza I held, faded away as she spoke. Admittedly, my preferred period of Elvis is the Sun Records, and pre-Army RCA years, and I didn't know her mother at all, so she could have liked the 1970s jumpsuit Elvis (a picture of him from that period still hangs on the wall in their kitchen.)

Our conversation continued, and it mostly revolved around music. Also revolving around us was the waiter who kept coming by to ask if everything was okay. Now, I know that servers are supposed to do that to provide good service, but I can't tell you the number of times that wait staff would come specifically by our table, asking if everything was okay, possibly because we looked so unique. It's that sixth sense, that one you get having had a congenital disability.

Anyway, we were both scoring points on the others' checklists but had also just talked about fairly superficial things. There was no talk of romance or anything, as it was a first date, after all.

I also asked her about her disability. When she said osteogenesis imperfecta, my scientific brain went to work: osteo meaning bone, genesis meaning first, imperfecta meaning, well, imperfect. As these words came out of my mouth, she simplified it for me: brittle bones; they break easily. She shared some of her backstory, and I did the same about my blindness.

The highlight of our first date was the moment when I offered her a taste of my beer. It was a porter, and it wasn't the best. But all of the other things on the menu were light or wheat beers, and I was a dark beer guy.

She accepted the request, and I said, "Um … how are we gonna do this?" This was a phrase that became a rallying cry of sorts that we used until our last moments together.

"Well, just push it over here. There's nothing in front of you."

I began scooting the glass across the table. It was a standard table for four that could accommodate a wheelchair and a dog. Not wanting to spill, I moved slowly and kept scooting the glass according to her instructions: "Closer … closer … little more … almost …" I couldn't help myself and burst out, "How short are you?!"

Her response was priceless: "Numbers don't matter! Okay! Got it!"

By this time, my torso was leaning across the table with my arm outstretched, as if I were being passed the baton in a track and field event. I felt her grab the glass, and I let go. There was a pregnant pause while I held this awkward position, and she took a sip.

"Yeah, that's pretty shitty. Here ya go!" She shoved it back at me as much as her little arms would allow.

I busted out laughing. I hadn't laughed that hard in a long time, and I really liked this girl's honesty. I wish I could've seen her facial expression. What I loved about that moment specifically is that I knew she wouldn't beat around any sort of bush when it came to her opinions. There was rarely any sugarcoating with Priscilla Carlson. Anybody, and everybody, knew exactly how she felt.

From the previous experiences I had had with girls, most of them would listen to a piece of music I would play them or have a sip of beer and say with a sort of unconvincing sweet tone, "Oh ... um ... that's interesting."

Mostly, they didn't give a shit about the music or the beer at all, but were just trying to be nice. Not Priscilla. I knew right from the get-go that she didn't like that beer. She did learn to like dark beer in later years; one of her favorites was a coffee stout that I still have a bottle of.

As any gentleman would do, I picked up the tab, something she found endearing later in our relationship. After I paid the tab, she suggested we go to an Asian tea place named Lollycup, for boba. Bobas are little tapioca balls put into tea. It can either be served as a hot or cold drink. They have a chewy consistency when cold, and a soft but still kind of chewy texture when served hot. It's an acquired taste.

I went along with her suggestion because I was enjoying myself. I hadn't really enjoyed myself on a date in I-don't-know-how long.

She later told me, "I didn't want the date to end, so I suggested Lollycup because it was the only place I knew on the Hill besides The Sink." The Hill is the hangout place for University of Colorado college kids. It contains retail shops and numerous restaurants, including The Sink.

The night was beautiful for March, so we went and got boba. The place was pretty much empty. In that moment, I did something neither of us really expected; I held her hand. I remember thinking to myself, "If she shoves her hand away and says no, then at least I tried." She didn't move her hand away.

Contrary to popular belief, blind people do not feel a person's face to "see" what they look like. Sighted people are so face-oriented, that it's assumed, stereotypically, that blind people are as well. This is not the case. Sometimes, holding someone's hand gives an indication of their features, and in this case, I was able to get a better sense of her small stature.

Priscilla later told me, "I remember thinking that you were the only guy I knew who didn't freak out about me being brittle. Most guys thought my hand or body would turn to dust and that I was too delicate to touch. You holding my hand kind of shocked me, but I liked it. A lot."

We sat there drinking our tea while I still held her hand. It was small and frail, but that was to be expected if she had brittle bones. Her hand was delicate, with long fingers that could have played a piano or harp if they had the strength.

Her hand was resting on her leg, and for the rest of her life, she would claim that I groped her. Honestly, I don't remember feeling up her leg, but if I did, how else am I supposed to know what it looks like? It wasn't intentional if I did grope her. However, I bring this up because her reaction to it was pure Priscilla. Apparently, when she told her roommate, Teresa, about the date, that part of the conversation went something like this:

Priscilla: "I think I got groped on my date."

Teresa: "Priscilla! That's not cool, did you tell him to stop?"

Priscilla: "No! I kinda liked it!"

Eventually, the date had to end. But it was not without two incidents which I find to be priceless and exceedingly humorous. We had to throw our cups away in the trash can. I asked Priscilla to help me do this. She had never guided a blind person from one place to another, let alone help him or her throw something away in the trash can. Her directions to me as we walked up to the receptacle and I reached for it sounded something like:

"Okay, up a little … now to the right, I mean left, little too far, yeah … there, in there …"

Without realizing what I was saying, I couldn't help exclaiming, "You kind of suck at this."

Her response was a simple, "Shut up, it's my first time!"

We left the tea place and began walking when she told me she had no idea where she was going. I needed to take the dog out to the bathroom at a certain spot, and I knew where everything was on the Hill. I knew it like the back of my hand because I frequented it nearly every day to eat. As we began walking to where I needed to go, I held onto her wheelchair, and Katie walked beside us. I would have used Katie as a guide except I wanted to walk slower than we usually do. I began describing to Priscilla where we needed to go.

"Okay, you're going to go up the hill, across an alley, and then look for the ramp that goes to the underpass. Wait, you do realize you're letting a blind guy guide you around the Hill when you can see everything that's going on, right?"

She laughed. "Hey man, I don't know where I'm going, and you do, so there!" This was true, but it was an irony we would laugh about for the rest of our time together.

We said goodbye, and I gave her an awkward hug. I took the dog, and as we walked home, I remember thinking, well, that was really nice, but just treat her as a friend. Maybe she was just being nice letting me hold her hand. (I have had that happen before with other women and later found out that they really didn't want to hold my hand.) I did walk with a little more spring in my step, though.

Priscilla, for her part, had a far more delightful reaction and, as usual, wore her emotions on her sleeve. Right after our date, she had plans to go to Las Vegas with Teresa and Molly, two girlfriends in wheelchairs, and an able-bodied chaperone. After going home to her apartment and relating the dating experience to Teresa, they packed up and headed off for spring break vacation. I asked Priscilla what she was thinking while on that vacation.

"You ruined my spring break!" she said. "All I could think about was you and things that you would like or find interesting while I was in Vegas. Teresa and Molly told me to not be "that girl" who texted you about all of the things that I found interesting. I didn't want to look like a stalker or something."

I had teased her about not sending me drunken texts and being too drunk to dial me while playing the slot machines. She sent me one text throughout the entire trip, telling me that they went to the Beatles Revolution Hard Rock Cafe. I have since lost the original text, but I do remember that the first part went something to the effect of: "This is not a drunk text, but I am standing in front of the Revolution ..."

As for me, I had to write papers during my spring break. I also got a really bad cold. Priscilla came back from Las Vegas with a cold which developed into a sinus infection. This became yet another pattern that would repeat for the rest of her life. We saw each other again and decided to go to a jazz concert. The concert was nice, but we were both very sick. Despite that, we wanted to see each other.

Things moved quickly. We really hit it off, and conversation was so easy between us. Our next date involved going to Best Buy so that I could pick up a headset. I told her that this was probably a really lame date and apologized, but I did need a sighted person to help me.

She responded, "Are you kidding? I love Best Buy, let's go!" So, we went.

After that, I went back to her place for the first time. Our sexual explorations began that evening.

CHAPTER FIVE

The Chinese Horoscope

We spent the rest of the semester doing what most college couples do: taking classes, studying, and spending way too much time together. The latter made the former much more difficult to do, but we really didn't care.

Priscilla received her driver's license in May. She took her driver's test, which she thought she had failed (does anybody really think they actually aced their driver's test on the first try?) and subsequently drove herself to the doctor to get medication for the sinus infection that she had developed. What a way to indoctrinate one into fully driving without anybody sitting in the car next to them telling them what to do! Congratulations, you have a license, here's a prescription, now drive yourself home and get better. She spent the next three days in bed, and we talked a little bit on the phone.

I was sending her songs by that point—those I thought were meaningful or that I just liked. She did the same. When she took her driving test, I sent her the Weird Al parody of the song "She Drives Me Crazy," called "She Drives Like Crazy." This catered to Priscilla's love of '80s music and was just me being silly. She sent me the '50s song "26 miles to Santa Catalina," which I'd never heard before.

I soon met Priscilla's roommate, Teresa. She is Asian and speaks fluent Vietnamese. She also has OI and is in a power chair. She is a skinny twig. Priscilla was not. However, people often confused the two of them.

One day as we were getting off the bus, a woman exclaimed, "You're one of the sisters!"

Priscilla didn't know what to say to that except, "What?" and was thinking that the driver thought she and Teresa were nuns or something.

The woman clearly thought that Priscilla and Teresa were sisters, despite their size and racial difference. The problem is that people just look at the wheelchair. I have numerous stories of misidentification of Priscilla, as well as countless variants on how people thought her name was pronounced or spelled.

Anyway, I met Teresa at my favorite sandwich shop,

which I frequented at least three times a week. I had no idea what to expect. I found, sitting across from me, a squeaky-voiced small person who knew how to swear better than most people I had met who were ex-military. That was my first impression.

Fuck! This girl knows how to say fuck a lot!

At first, I found it annoying and thought her immature, but soon we would become good friends, partly because I stayed over at Priscilla's place all of the time.

I scored brownie points with Priscilla because Teresa did not like to eat leftovers. One of the first things Priscilla asked me when we entered her apartment was, "Do you like leftovers?" My response was, "Are you kidding? I live on leftovers, that was my childhood!" Score! Free food!

I also had a chance to meet Lisa, Priscilla's friend who had brought Priscilla out to Colorado. She, her husband Chris, and their friend Stacy owned a house. They had also adopted a daughter named Anese from Belize. She also had osteogenesis imperfecta and was six or seven at the time. I got along with all of them well enough. Lisa and I clashed on some things, but we both have very strong personalities and, well, I will admit I am a bit rough around the edges at times. I generally said what I felt, and sometimes it wasn't the nicest. I credit Priscilla for mellowing me out a bit. And there's probably something to be said about getting older and wiser.

While taking classes, I had been looking into something to do over the summer of 2011. I have always been interested in old recordings, and enjoyed restoring records. My goal was to get to the Library of Congress Recorded Sound Division, which is located in Culpeper, Virginia. Instead, I stumbled on a blog about sound films. These were an early attempt in about 1930 by the General Electric Company to combine audio and video. The so-called talkies had been around since 1927 when Al Jolson played a song in the otherwise silent movie *The Jazz Singer*. My understanding was that it was a phonograph record that was played over the rest of the movie. Thus, talking movies were still in their relative infancy.

Thomas Edison was eighty-three at the time, and would die a year later in 1931. One of his engineers developed a machine to record music off the radio that they hoped to eventually marry to video footage. The project did not gain momentum and was quickly scrapped.

However, at the Schenectady Museum of Innovation and Science in New York, the canisters containing these old films, along with the blueprints for how to make the machine, were found in the General Electric archives. One of the archivists at the museum actually re-created the machine as best he could. They then ran the reels of film through the machine and digitized what they had.

Not expecting a response, I wrote an email to the blog contact, looking for some kind of job to do. I received a reply the next morning that was simple and to the point. We could probably work out some sort of internship. Okay, I was getting onto something.

From about April 1 to June 1, 2011, I developed a plan to go to this museum. There were possibly three hundred recordings to be digitized. There were also several jukeboxes full of records, and nobody knew what was on them. I knew I wouldn't get paid for it but was hoping these people had connections that might lead somewhere.

After searching around, I found an apartment I could rent for two months, which was a very difficult task because most people wanted a three- or six-month lease. One guy agreed to take me on when I told him what I was doing. The place came unfurnished, so I rented furniture from a Rent-A-Center close by. On June 1, I left Colorado on a plane bound for Albany, New York. It was just Katie and me and a suitcase. I had no idea what my accommodations would be like, I didn't know anybody except the guy at the museum who seemed rather shy and awkward, even over the phone, and I had no groceries.

My parents were shocked and quite concerned that I was doing this trip all by myself. My dad reminded me that I wasn't going to have anybody helping me shop. I used his old adage: "Well, I'll just make it up." That was exactly what I did.

Priscilla helped me prepare for the trip. I asked if she could help me go to the mall and pick out clothes to wear. I had no idea if I was going to be near anybody at the front of the museum or in the view of people, so I figured I should get some nice clothing.

After proposing this, her response was one which we quoted often, "Wait, you mean I get to dress you and pick things out for you, and don't have to pay? Okay! You're like my real live Ken doll!"

Oh lord. What had I asked for? We stuck to pretty neutral colors so that everything matched easily enough. This included three pairs of brown slacks of the exact same shade. Some might think this redundantly redundant, but I found it quite useful because I didn't have to worry about what shirt was going with which pants. I still wear those slacks today.

Priscilla was busy working with the student group in which we had originally met about a year earlier. She was now managing it and pushing for advocacy. She was also working on her journalism classes along with the political science courses. Her summer also involved an internship at the news radio station KOA in Denver. As an aspiring journalist, this was a big step in the right direction for her. KOA broadcasts ninety-nine percent of the Rockies games (until the Broncos play starting in September, and then they occasionally move to another station in the Denver area), so I was all for it. Plus, I knew this would get her some great experience.

We planned on going to Washington, D.C., together the following summer. I really wanted to work at that Library of Congress Recorded Sound Division, despite the fact that it was quite far from the District of Columbia itself.

On our last night together before I left for New York, we did something I never thought we would get a chance to do—we went to the Brown Palace. This is a fancy hotel in downtown Denver, circa 1882. Out of sheer compulsion, curiosity, and just plain lunacy, we asked them if they had any accessible rooms. What the hell, we didn't think we'd get any since it was such an old place. Turns out we were wrong. There is a suite which is accessible—if you can afford $550 a night.

Needless to say, we balked. Katie the dog sat there looking around and probably wondering why we were taking so long checking in. Maybe it was the dog, maybe it was the fact that we made such a striking couple, or maybe it was just sheer luck, but the manager and the desk clerk had a whispered conversation and agreed to give us the room for less than half of the quoted price. We turned around, looked at each other for about three seconds, and said, "Okay!"

While we were staying there, room service brought us "dog amenities." They had said at the front desk that we could get a dog bed, a bowl, and other dog items. Little did we know exactly what the dog bed was. When they delivered it, I answered the door while Priscilla was in the bedroom.

"Bring it in here, Dave. The bed." The frame was metal. It was a mini replica of the iron human beds that the hotel had. Okay, it must be made out of steel, right? WRONG! It was made out of iron! I stumbled into the bedroom, holding this thing around my knees because it was so heavy and giving Priscilla a look like I was about to give birth. I set it down, wiped the perspiration off of my brow, and said, "There! Happy? That fucker's made of iron! God dammit, you tryin' to kill me?"

Katie, meanwhile, was tearing open the plastic baggy of treats that had been taped to the bed. We could barely get her to sleep in it, but we did get a picture of it. So at the Brown Palace, we had a mixture of helpful and unhelpful things going on. They made the suite accessible for us both physically and financially, but when it came time for the dog bed, well … they didn't quite understand just how I was going to carry it into the bedroom, not having the visual clue of it being cast-iron before I picked it up. They just dropped it off, and I had the privilege to bring it into the bedroom by myself. In fairness, I don't think the person who delivered the dog bed spoke English very well, and therefore, there was a communication gap. Life is complicated—there is no cut and dried way to always communicate or self-advocate. Sometimes you just live and learn, live and teach, live and laugh.

The next day, after a four-hour flight, Katie and I arrived in New York. I took a cab to my apartment and discovered that I had forgotten to pack toilet paper and dog food. The furniture people came in, and I befriended one of the movers who helped me get much-needed groceries—the absolute bare essentials, which of course included a six-pack of Blue Moon beer. I had to depend on my guide dog and all of the mobility skills at my disposal. But really, when the paws met the sidewalk, I knew I would figure it out. So, when it came time for basic things like buying groceries, I took a cab. I asked for sighted assistance when I went into the store to help me get what I needed. Asking for assistance is how I oriented myself in a new city, a new store, and with complete strangers.

I spent the next two months digitizing old recordings from the General Electric archives. We got off to a slow start because the turntable they had was grinding to a halt. Luckily, they had some grant money left over, so I did some research and bought a far nicer, variable-speed, mechanical-drive turntable. This is the type of equipment audio restoration professionals use.

Priscilla and I spoke almost nightly. We even emailed things back and forth to each other. If I found a particularly hilarious recording, I would cut out a part of it and send it to her. If she found a news story and was working on recording it for the radio station, she would send me a clip of that. I also managed to do a little bit of sightseeing and also went to Yankees Stadium to catch a Yankees versus Rockies game. The Rockies lost, which was no surprise that year.

During one of our early phone conversations when we were both sick as dogs, Priscilla asked, "So, when's your birthday?"

Automatically, I responded, "November 16, 1986. Why?"

She said, "Well, I was born February 20, 1978."

My response was, "Oh, okay so you're ..." *quick Dave, do the math.* My ape brain was on slow that day. "So, you're 33." It wasn't a question, it was a statement.

She said, a little shakily, "Yeah, so uh, how does it feel to be dating a cougar?"

"A what?" I knew a "cougar" was a mountain lion, and I definitely knew Priscilla was a human, so this term did not register in Dave's dictionary of known slang of the English language. Maybe she used the term incorrectly? All I could think of to say was, "You mean, like Freddy Krueger?"

It was the only thing I could think of that rhymed with this new word. Then I thought again. Wait! A cougar is an animal, oh maybe she means ... then I said something without thinking about the words coming out of my mouth, "Hun, I don't really care about your Chinese horoscope, if that's what you mean?"

My rationale for this was simple. In my mind, there was the year of the rat, the monkey, the bear, so why couldn't there be a year for the cougar? Nineteen seventy-eight must be the year of the cougar.

She laughed. Now it was her turn to be confused, "My what? You've never heard that word before?"

"Uh, no." I felt really fucking stupid! I explained my Chinese horoscope logic to her, and she laughed again, the full-throated laugh that always made her chair shake.

"No, silly, a cougar is a woman who goes out with younger men."

"Oh …" was all I could say. "Well, uh, I mean, that's fine, doesn't make a difference to me."

I later found out what was going on in Priscilla's mind when I gave her my birthdate:

I thought, when we went on our first date, he must be in his late twenties or early thirties, maybe around my age? I mean, he was mature and handsome, so when he gave me his birthday and I heard '1986,' I thought, 'Oh fuck! He's twenty-four?!' Later, when I told my brother, Dion, how old Dave was, he was like, "Whooo! Priscilla! Robbing the cradle much?"

The short answer was, no, the cradle had been robbed when I had my first serious relationship with a woman who was three years older. I had never dated anyone younger than me. Guess those cougars sure had their claws in me after all. RARRRRRR! During my internship, there were times when I felt lonely, but it was nice to know that my cougar Priscilla was just a phone call away.

One day, I came home from a deli, which made the biggest ham sandwich I'd ever eaten, and received a call from my bank. They asked if I was in Iowa. I told them that no, I was in Schenectady and had been since June 1. My credit card number had been stolen, and I had two weeks to go before my internship ended, so I was forced to borrow and pay back when I could to make ends meet. The replacement card was rushed to me, at the wrong address, and then again, at the right address, four days before I left. Always an adventure.

Priscilla agreed to pick me up from the airport in her car. We wanted to see each other quite badly by that point. I had gone over the scene several times in my mind: I would come out of the jetway with Katie by my side, and Priscilla would be waiting at the gate (she got a gate pass). I told myself that there was nothing to worry about and pictured a nice suave entrance. However, when I landed, I told the crew that Katie and I did not need help. We left the airplane, walking at a brisk pace, as we usually did, and WHAM! Katie ran me into one of those customer-service signs that stands just outside of the jetway. She had seen Priscilla and turned into a wagging rocket! Meanwhile, the sign clattered to the floor with a resounding metallic crash, and I went with it. I corrected Katie on instinct (the motion that one makes when a guide dog misbehaves) and got up on my knees. A hush fell over the passengers in the terminal as Priscilla asked, "Oh God! Are you okay?"

I didn't know what else to do. I just started laughing. I guess Joe Cool wasn't so cool after all. My body was fine, but my ego was a bit bruised thanks to my well-meaning, furry, meet-and-greet party. Laughter can make some of the worst situations into some of the most memorable.

CHAPTER SIX

The Enterprise

In writing this story, I have to mention a very important character. He is vital to the continuance of the plot from 2011 to 2017. His wisdom faltered at times, but overall, he was critically important to Priscilla. I found out shortly after we started dating that I would have to play second fiddle to this character, no matter how hard I tried to overcome our differences. His strength and abilities were far beyond mine. He had power and lots and lots of drive.

I'm not talking about another person, no, not at all. I'm talking about Priscilla's minivan. Yes, you read that right—her minivan. She was able to drive with the use of a very expensive, very cool, and very customized system of machinery and computers. It took her four years to get it. The Division of Vocational Rehabilitation (a government agency that helps people with disabilities to find employment) always has to have the details of requests for funding spelled out so they know exactly where their money is going. This $80,000 adaptation to a minivan would allow Priscilla to find gainful employment and chase stories as a news reporter.

Priscilla had to be smart about her word choice on the funding application, and her counselor had to guide her through all of the steps necessary to attain the funding, not including the van itself. Most people just simply walk into a dealership and spend what feels like four years to get a car and the appropriate financing.

Getting her license included being placed on a waiting list for a cognitive assessment to make sure she had the mental capacity to drive. She went back-and forth with the assessment person, trying to schedule a time— a process that took nine months to figure out. Priscilla also needed to complete seventy hours of behind-the-wheel training to learn how to drive and master the complex computer system, which was an adaptation to the minivan.

I don't drive, but I do wonder how much better driving could be if everyone had to go through seventy hours of training and a cognitive assessment. Nonetheless, Priscilla was finally awarded her license on May 7, 2011.

Allow me to describe the majesty that was The Enterprise, a 2010 Dodge Grand Caravan SXT. It had a dropped floor, meaning that it was made for someone in a wheelchair to use. This also meant that the floor was literally an inch or two from the ground. Because of this, we hit a lot of potholes and endured a lot of loud scraping noises on speed bumps. But I digress.

The Enterprise was silver and had been, oddly enough, a rental van from the Enterprise Rent-A-Car company. It had about eight thousand miles on it when Priscilla got it, and it cost $20,000 prior to modifications.

Getting the adaptations, and her parents' belief in her driving abilities, was another matter entirely. The first time she went to a dealership specializing in accessible vehicles, she was confronted by a man who told her, in the following way, that she needed a full-sized van, despite her request for a minivan. She described the salesman as saying something like, "Well, little lady, I'm just not sure how you're gonna do that. You need a full-sized van with a lift. A minivan won't work."

Okay, first of all, NEVER call Priscilla Carlson "little lady." Not only is it condescending to a person in a wheelchair, P's (sometimes I called her Priscilla; sometimes I called her P) demeanor is not one to be trifled with. She might be small in stature, but that's it.

Next, there was no way she was going to get a full-sized van. Those are the types of vans that completely fill up the accessible parking spots at stores and have a lift that comes out the back or side of the van to bring the wheelchair in and out. One of her friends had a van like that, and her lift had gotten stuck more than once. If something like that happened to Priscilla, how could she call for help? Suppose she was in a parking garage and didn't have cell reception? Or worse still, the lift moved too fast, and she cracked a bone when it descended? I've heard of that happening too. Needless to say, her first encounter with an accessible van dealer was not a rousing success. She knew there were people out there with minivans with ramps.

So, what did the car look like, and how did it function? It had a computer system comprised of eight hard drives. These drives were backups of one primary unit, so that if something went wrong, the backups would be ready to take over. The computer was housed in a large box between the passenger and driver's seats. There was a joystick control shaped like a T that controlled the brake and gas. There was also a flat wheel with a knob that served as the steering wheel. Lastly, there was a small touchscreen that controlled the entire operation, including the windshield wipers, air-conditioning and heat, the horn, and the shifting of gears.

There was just one small problem. This time the problem was literally small—Priscilla's height and reach. She was too small to see over the dash of the car, and the steering wheel was too big for her to see through, so the person who installed the equipment devised an ingenious idea. First, he replaced the regular steering wheel with a smaller racing wheel, like the kind used in the Formula One races. This way, when Priscilla turned the flat wheel, the smaller steering wheel would rotate and give her a visual of where her tires were going. Second, and most brilliant of all, was that the engineer/mechanic designed what's called a reverse power pan. This was a platform that was originally designed to lower dirt bikes into a truck. The bike would be placed on the platform, and it would lower down and move backward into the bed of the truck.

Well, what if that process were reversed? What if the power pan were to move up and forward instead of down and backward? Maybe then Priscilla could drive from her chair and see over the dashboard. It worked! It was magical to see that thing lift a chair that weighed anywhere from 240–370 pounds, depending on which wheelchair she was in, as well as Priscilla's small body up to the height of a "normal" driver, if not a bit higher. Thankfully, she had other options because the first dealer wasn't the only game in town, at least not until they bought out every other one around the area.

The Enterprise became her biggest source of pride, and she was ready and willing to show it off to anybody who wanted to see it. I don't blame her, considering how many years it took to get it, and she was a true self-advocate through the entire process.

Priscilla always called The Enterprise "him" or "he," and I asked her why: "Wait, are you saying your car has male parts?"

Her response was something we relayed back and forth quite a bit from that day forth: "Well, guys always talk about their cars and say, 'Isn't she a beauty?' and shit like that, so I figured my Enterprise would be a 'he.'"

Sometimes, she would walk by the car and intone, "If I could, I would just reach out and pet your fenders."

That always made me laugh because it's just such a bizarre statement. But yes, I was second in line to the God damn minivan. Despite that, I used to tell people, "I only started dating Priscilla because she had a minivan," to which she would respond, on cue, "I only started dating him because of his dog."

Both the car and Katie got plenty of attention from both of us. Both were not without their own health problems and setbacks, but they both performed admirably well until the very last.

CHAPTER SEVEN

Slippery Slopes

The morning of November 4, 2011, was cold. A storm had whipped through the area a few nights before. This was not an uncommon occurrence this time of year. But it was a big storm, the kind that leaves cars stranded and snow tumbling from the sky like rocks rather than flakes. Priscilla and I were getting ready for school, as usual.

We were ready to go, but Priscilla wanted to try to start the minivan with the auto-start. It wasn't working. That damn thing never worked, but it was cold, and we figured we'd give it a shot. I had Katie harnessed up, my backpack was on, and everything was ready.

Priscilla said, "Go ahead and wait here, I'll be back." She left.

I waited.

And waited.

Then I thought I heard a strangled cry. Something was not right. I left Katie in the entryway and very slowly walked outside. The air was chilled, humid, and damp. It stung my face and made me shiver even though I wore a jacket and carried a bulky backpack.

I paused, looking around, listening intently for a noise, then I heard Priscilla call my name in the most anguished cry I had ever heard her utter: "DAVE?!"

"YEAH?" The minivan was in front of me and to my left in the usual parking spot. Then came the words that still haunt me on a daily basis.

"DAVE! HURRY! COME HERE QUICK! I FELL OUT OF MY CHAIR!"

I cannot describe the fear that gripped me at that moment. I had known something wasn't right, but this was NOT what I wanted it to be. My blood ran cold. It didn't help that it was cold outside too. What could I do? I ran. The site was one that you didn't need to be sighted to find. What I found was not good.

There was Priscilla, her van running, laying under the car in the neighboring parking spot. She was on her stomach, her legs twisted and bent like pretzels. Her right leg was up by her chin. She screamed, "Call 911!"

For the first time in my life, and I hoped the last, I pulled out my phone and called the three numbers that no one ever wants to dial. I am very glad Priscilla was conscious, because I realized with horror that I didn't know the address of her apartment! I just knew I went there a lot! I can't tell you specifics of the call, just that I said my girlfriend had fallen out of her chair and had brittle bones, and we needed an ambulance as fast as possible.

Next, Priscilla told me the phone number to call her friend Lisa. I called and told her what had happened. Priscilla knew her legs were broken. I asked if I could help, but she said no because I wouldn't know how to move her.

Both the paramedics and the person who owned the car that Priscilla was under arrived at about the same time. I am sure that the looks on their faces mirrored each other. Neither of them knew what to do. Priscilla had to take charge. The paramedics slid something under Priscilla to get her off the ground. She was still in the prone position, and people of her size with OI of her type do NOT lie on their stomachs. Her lungs were being crushed by her body weight. Her wheelchair, thankfully, had brakes and stopped on the ramp. Otherwise, it could have killed her.

The chair had slipped on a patch of ice at the end of the minivan ramp. Priscilla had not been able to get the auto-start to work, so without thinking twice and wearing no seatbelt, she drove her wheelchair up the ramp and started the engine. She turned, went down the ramp, and the chair slipped. She had no way to stop her fall! She was top-heavy, her legs dead weight, so her torso tipped and down she went, landing on both of her thigh bones.

She had started the minivan like this before but had not thought about there being ice at the end of the ramp. The ramp folded into the side door area of the minivan, and the small piece of ice caught at the end of the ramp was enough to jar the chair and toss her small body out.

The paramedics asked who I was, and I answered, while Priscilla immediately added, "He's riding in the ambulance." Well, one thing was certain, she knew what she wanted, and she wanted me by her side. Thank God.

The hospital we went to first is one for which I will always have extreme disdain because of their treatment of Priscilla. The staff were not attentive, and did not seem to think Priscilla nor I could speak for ourselves or had intelligence. Unfortunately, this is something that is far too common in society, but is more pronounced in high-stress medical fields. This was the first time I had ever been in an emergency medical situation of this magnitude. I had no idea what to expect. They didn't seem to care if I was Priscilla's boyfriend or not. What could I do as an advocate for her? In this case, I had to let Priscilla do the talking.

We came into the ER area, only to wait. Time and again, medical staff would walk by the gurney she was on, where she remained in the same painful position in which she had fallen, with her foot hanging off the table. Despite the screams she made every time someone accidentally bumped her foot, they wouldn't give her pain medication. This led to the worst screams I have ever heard anyone make. The painful anguish ripped through me like a knife cuts through flesh. At one point, they had hit her leg enough times that Priscilla screamed, "STOP HITTING MY FUCKING LEG, THIS HURTS!"

Rather than compassion or help, the nurse curtly replied, "You watch your language!" Okay, Priscilla had dropped an F-bomb, but, really? Language was the first thing on this nurse's mind, not trying to address the situation and saying something like, "Oh, I'm sorry, we'll try to move around your leg, so we don't hit you."

Nope, apparently foul language took over as principal antagonist. Did they stop hitting her leg? No! I just remember the screams and the pleading little voice asking for pain medication. I cannot recall why they wouldn't give it to her. They were trying to figure out her doctors and where she could go. This was not an impressive staff.

At this time in our lives, I had never spoken to her family in North Dakota, but we had planned to go out there for Thanksgiving. Nonetheless, I had to call them and tell them the news.

Cledith was in the field, farming. There was a lot of

noise, and he could hardly hear me. I had never spoken to the man, and now I had to tell him that his daughter had fallen and broken who-knows-how-many bones in her legs. Great way to meet your girlfriend's father, isn't it? It was the same with calling her brother, Dion. I'd never talked to him either, but someone had to tell her family.

What happened next seemed surreal, but it adds an element of humor to a frightening, gut-wrenching story. The doctors decided to transfer Priscilla to Denver's Children's Hospital. The orthopedic specialist, who was familiar with OI, would not be in until Monday, but Priscilla could wait there until then. He would make an exception to the age limit of eighteen which was normally imposed, because she didn't have a specific doctor for OI in Colorado.

Finally, she received some pain medication because they had to move her from the position she was in. Away we went in the ambulance, again. There I was, my girlfriend of seven months in the back being tended to by two paramedics, two more in front with me—one driving and the other supervising.

And then it hit me.

I had to pee.

I'm not talking having to pee like, "Oh hey, can we stop at the nearest gas station and get a soda, and I'll pee." I'm talking, "If I don't pee now, I will pee my pants!"

Oh God, not another bump! One more and I was

done for. My bladder was surely going to burst due to all the stress of dealing with pressure I had never felt before. I had no clue what I had been doing, and oh, this was not good! But wait, I was in an ambulance. Surely, they'd seen it all before and were prepared for this situation, right?

I had to do something. "Um, ma'am, I'm not sure how to ask, but I have to pee really, really badly, and soon, or I will piss my pants. Is there something you can give me to pee in?"

One paramedic asked the other, while I sat now in considerable pain, but inwardly amused at the irony of the situation. They had a bio bag, a plastic bag for, well, waste, I guess. They handed it to me, but that was only half the battle. I'd never peed in a moving vehicle, sitting down in a seat. Even in an airplane, I could stand and aim. Plus, I had to make sure my bladder wasn't going to explode. So, as carefully as I could, I unbuckled my seatbelt and, modesty be damned, unzipped.

Then the driver said what I had hoped to hear, "Don't worry, I've seen it all, heard it all, smelled it all."

That was just the invitation my body needed, but what if I wasn't in the bag? I did a check three times to make sure I was aiming at the inside of the bag. I have never had a urinary tract infection, but the pain I felt when I emptied my bladder in that ambulance must be close to what it feels like. I nearly screamed aloud because my bladder was so full. I thanked the Lord above for two things in that moment: first, that I was a male, and second, that I didn't miss or spill. I handed the bag back to the paramedic behind me and breathed a sigh of relief. We were only halfway to the hospital!

Why am I bringing up this story? Because it was one of those perfect storm situations in which I had to look at what was going on and say to myself, "Figures, Priscilla is screaming in pain, and all I can do is pee like a drunk Rockies fan at Coors Field with two down in the fourteenth inning and bases loaded for the home team." It was adding insult to injury in what was already turning out to be a hellish day.

The next day and a half were a blur. As anyone who has been confronted with a crisis situation will tell you, things felt like they were happening in slow motion. I remember Priscilla getting splints, and I remember people taking Katie home with them. I can remember sending emails to teachers at my musicology program, telling them that I was in a state of emergency. I also remember calling Dion, and answering other people on Facebook who were asking me how Priscilla was doing.

What is important to remember is that Priscilla was in a children's hospital, but she was thirty-three years old. No one knew how to take care of someone with OI, much less someone who was an adult. It was the weekend, and the staff was a skeleton crew. The goal was to make it through the weekend until Monday when the pediatric orthopedist would show up. It was a hurry-up-and-wait game. A few X-rays were taken. Otherwise, Priscilla was resting in one position for most of Friday and Saturday. The painkillers were taking effect, and she was in a haze.

I had to step up and be an advocate for Priscilla who was under the influence of a morphine drip. I still was very clueless and in shock from the whole situation, but I knew that the physical therapist resident should not have been talking to me or anybody in the dismissive manner in which she was. For example, she asked me if Priscilla was able to transfer herself from the bed to the wheelchair on her own. To me, the question seemed so absurd. It seemed anyone with sense, let alone sight, could see that was not going to be possible. She had two broken legs. A healthy twenty-year-old male could not transfer himself in such a condition.

"No, I don't believe so," was my shocked response.

"Well, if she can do that by the end of the weekend, she'll be fine."

Did she read her fucking chart? I told the nurse that her behavior was beyond unacceptable because she needed to know that you don't talk to people like that. Now, I will admit, I have no idea if she talked to everyone like she was God's gift to physical therapy, but I felt like she was talking specifically to me and, in effect, to Priscilla that way. Little did I know how much talking I would have to do myself in the weeks and months ahead for someone I truly loved.

Hospitals are breeding grounds for condescension, ignorance, and sometimes just plain stupidity that can cost someone's life. We almost lost Priscilla during this ordeal. At one point, Priscilla was given a dose of Valium that was too much for her body weight, and she began foaming at the mouth while sleeping. Her parents and her friend Nikki were in the room with me, and they asked the nurse how much Valium Priscilla had been given. The nurse responded they had given her the dose for somebody who was 120 pounds. Everybody was shocked and horrified.

Nikki's response was, "LOOK AT HER!" Priscilla was about half that weight. She woke up, and everything was fine for her, but her family and Nikki were definitely tired because they had spent the entire night watching her to make sure that she was still breathing. To the doctors and nurses reading this, please double-check the patient's weight before administering medications.

When Saturday evening arrived, I was doing nothing but watching P to make sure she was okay. The nurse came in and asked if she wanted any food. "We have Jell-O, and apple juice, and crackers, or I could get someone to make you something from the kitchen," she said.

Priscilla requested the Jell-O, and in hospital time

(I am convinced hospitals operate on their own time zone), it was finally delivered in one of those little plastic cups. Great, they brought the Jell-O, but no one considered how she would eat it.

I waited for the word. Then, in a sad, pitiful, heart-wrenching voice that I would always remember, Priscilla said, "Dave, can you get me some Jell-O?"

I smiled, trying not to let the tears show. At that moment, she sounded like the little kid who just wanted one cookie from the cookie jar ... just one ... please? I was sure the look on her face was as pitiful as her voice. Picture the scene: There's me, totally blind, holding a Jell-O cup and a spoon. Then there's Priscilla, lying on her back, maybe leaning a bit forward, in a hospital bed, her legs wrapped in splints, an IV drip in her arm. Yet again, the question crossed both our minds, "Okay, how are we going to do this?"

I took off the plastic top and scooped some of the jiggly slippery stuff onto the spoon. That was one-third of the battle. Now, I had to find her mouth. I set the cup on the side table and proceeded to clumsily find her mouth, based on where I heard her breathing. Slowly, she parted her lips, and I inserted the spoon with the sticky gelatin on it. She licked my hand and managed to get some of the Jell-O on her tongue. It was more like she licked the essence of the Jell-O that was on my fingertips, as I had to make sure the spoon went into her mouth, and ensure the Jell-O didn't fall from it. We laughed. Lord, we laughed, as much as she could, given her morphine-induced state.

I tried again. Spoon. Jell-O cup. Spoon to mouth. Open mouth. Tongue and lips accept sticky goo. Finally, after the fourth or so attempt, I said, "Okay, this is not working. Can I just use my fingers?"

She replied softly, "Yeah. Yeah, that's fine."

I tossed the spoon aside, scooped up the cherry Jell-O by hand, and fed it to her, much the same way you would hand-feed a kitten. Her lips parted, her tongue came out, and licked what I had in my hand. It was, and still remains, one of the fondest memories I have of our time together. And I will never think of Jell-O the same again. Hand-fed, to the woman I had fallen in love with, no matter how injured she was. How that injury would develop, within mere hours, was to change all of our lives, forever.

CHAPTER EIGHT

Slippery Strokes

At 3:30 on Sunday morning, November 6, 2011, I woke up suddenly in Priscilla's hospital room. I felt a sudden jolt to wakefulness, as if my brain had sensed that something was wrong. I heard Priscilla talking and asked her what was going on. Her response sounded like mumbling.

"What was that, Sweetheart?" Again, I heard her but couldn't understand a word she was saying. I told her as much and said that I needed to go get the nurse. I didn't have a cane or a dog, so I just walked out of the room and listened for talking. I ran down to the end of the hall and told them that something was wrong, that they needed to attend to Priscilla. We all rushed back into the room, and the nurse asked, in a syrupy sweet voice common to Children's Hospital, "What's wrong, Priscilla?"

Again, nobody could understand her. They started asking her questions, "Are you in pain? Do you need water?"

Nobody could figure out why we couldn't understand her. Then she let out the most piteous, anguished cry I had ever heard. It still gives me chills to think about that noise. I had no idea what was going on, but I knew that something was not right.

The nurses told me that they were going to have to move her to University Hospital, which was just across the street. During all of this, they kept asking Priscilla what was wrong. All of a sudden, she wet the bed. The nurse exclaimed, "Oh! You had to pee!"

It was truly a mortifying scene for Priscilla. She didn't remember it, but she had wet the bed the day before because nobody had moved her due to her pain and splinted legs. There were "chucks," a type of pad to absorb urine and other liquids underneath her.

To transfer her, they had to move her onto a gurney and roll her to the ambulance that would take us to University Hospital. It took about an hour and a half to get everything ready for the short trip. While we waited, the nurse closest to the foot of the bed decided it would be a good idea to read Priscilla some of the cards that people had left for her. She began to open them up and read aloud wishes, such as, "Hope you get well soon. We love you." and "You're the greatest!" and "Your legs will heal in no time! Keep staying strong!"

Then the nurse came upon the card that two of Priscilla's friends had left her. I think it was from Teresa and her able-bodied friend Jenna. On one side of the card, it said in very large, bold letters, "PRISCILLA!!!" On the other side, in even larger letters, it just said, "FUCK!!!!!!!" There was a pause as I heard the paper being shifted. Then the nurse simply said, in her sweet young voice, "Oh, I can't read that one."

I laughed out loud because I knew exactly which one it was. You have to take humor where you can find it in a stressful and possibly life-threatening situation.

The nurses helped me pack up my things into a bag, and then very slowly and gingerly, they picked Priscilla up and moved her onto a gurney. I was tired, but more than that, I was scared out of my mind. Walking from her room to the elevator seemed like the longest walk of my life. They put me in the front of the ambulance just like they had done when they transported us to Children's Hospital. Luckily, this time I did not have to pee like a racehorse! The ride was only across a small street, but again it seemed like hours were going by. I heard the radio of the paramedic who was driving us. She picked it up and said the words that made my blood run ice cold, "We have a possible stroke victim coming to the ER, stand by."

I responded with, "A stroke?"

Her response was simple and flat-toned. "That's what we think it is."

I felt all of the color drain from my face. The panic and terror that set in was like nothing I had experienced. We got out of the ambulance, and they took Priscilla into the hospital. They led me to a waiting room. In the condescending tone that they seem to have for everybody with a disability, they told me, "We're going to leave you here and do some tests on Priscilla, okay?" I hear this tone in every hospital. People also usually speak very loudly and slowly because they think I'm deaf as well as blind.

So, I waited for about ten minutes or so before somebody came out and delivered the news that made my blood go from cold to pure ice. "Priscilla has had a massive stroke on the left side of her brain. It looks like it is a few hours old, so there is nothing we can do to try and stop it except wait for the swelling to go down. She is in the intensive care unit and you can see her in a little bit."

The only thing I could think of to say was, "Okay, thank you for letting me know, I will start calling people."

My mouth was as dry as Phoenix in the summertime when there is a water shortage. I first called Lisa and woke her up. I told her that Priscilla had had a stroke and heard her wake up Chris to tell him. I asked if she could call Priscilla's parents because I didn't know them that well and if she could come down as soon as possible. Then I called my parents. I had started crying by then. When my father and mother got on the phone, I told them that Priscilla had had a stroke. My father's immediate reaction was very pragmatic, "Will she live?"

That thought hadn't crossed my mind and sent me further into panic. He did not mean it in a hurtful way; it was just a knee-jerk reaction.

Through tears, I simply said, "I don't know."

My mother asked if they should come down. I began to cry harder and said, "If you want …" They showed up about forty-five minutes later.

The nurses led me to Priscilla. I said hello to her, and she said, "Okay." It was a mechanical sounding response which made me realize that she could not speak. The only thing that she could say was, "Okay." The word would come out at odd times and make no sense according to the context of the conversation.

I was a mess. I remember that when Lisa and Diane showed up, Diane gave me a big hug, and I sobbed uncontrollably. I will never forget that. I was crying when my mother arrived, and she asked me to stop, most likely because she was about to cry, too. Other people came as the morning went on. Lisa had called Priscilla's parents in North Dakota, and they were coming as soon as possible. Around nine in the morning, my parents and Lisa said that I should go home. I said that I wanted to stay with Priscilla. They told me that I needed to get some sleep because I'd been up since three-thirty. Begrudgingly, I left and went back to my parent's place. I was shaking with fear and so scared about everything that had happened. I did sleep, waking up around five that evening. I went back to the hospital that night. Nothing had changed.

The next morning, I met Priscilla's parents for the first time. I shook her father's hand while standing in the ICU. Her mother was sick with a cold and wanted to stay away. I told Cledith that this was not the ideal place to have a first introduction since we had planned on coming for Thanksgiving. I had a doctor's appointment that day, so I had to leave, but I promised I would come back. By that time, Priscilla had begun to say "Yes" and "No," which was a marked improvement from the day before.

During the time that I was with Priscilla's parents, there had been talk about what to do with Priscilla because of the broken bones and the stroke. Children's Hospital was not equipped to handle a thirty-three-year-old woman, even though she was the size of a small child. Conversely, University Hospital was not equipped to handle an adult woman who was the size of a small child and had eight broken bones, but they could handle the same woman who had had a stroke.

In the end, doctors from both sides came over to discuss the situation. I spoke with the neurologist who informed me that the stroke was on the left side of the brain. Priscilla had lost the ability to communicate, and most likely to read and to write, which were all functions of the left hemisphere. Her right side was paralyzed, and they weren't sure how much movement she would ever have on the right again. I do recall one moment in the hospital when she was trying to get to her phone and realized she couldn't read it. She threw it across the bed in sheer anger. To help P communicate, her friend Nikki designed flashcards that she could use to answer yes or no questions. The system worked well.

As I said earlier, the doctors knew nothing about working with somebody who had brittle bones. For some inexplicable reason, they tried to put in an arterial line (a port to give medication) and a catheter at the same time. Why they decided to do these extremely painful operations at once, I will never know. I was not there for this but was told that some people had to leave because Priscilla's screams of pain were too much for them to handle. The catheter never worked properly, which I found out later when I visited her that Monday evening.

Priscilla slowly gained the ability to say more words, although I don't recall what those words were. I do remember Lisa standing next to her bed. When Priscilla's parents were out of earshot, she said, "I just want you to say a fucking sentence."

We all chuckled at that and began to try and figure out when Priscilla would say something that resembled a sentence.

The most poignant moment occurred when we were all gathered around her bed, including her mother, who was feeling better by that point. We had gone to the gift shop downstairs at the hospital with my sister, and we had found a little teddy bear to give to Priscilla as a gift from me. It was just something cute that we thought might cheer her up a little, as much as she could be cheered up in the given situation. I gave her the teddy bear, and she began to cry.

Much to my astonishment, with everyone around, she said in a soft, whimpering voice, "Daaaaave."

A cacophony of bittersweet emotions ran through me. All I could say was, "She said my name?"

I was so shocked by this and was reminded instantly of a child who is just learning to say "Mama." I later found out from Darlene that my name was the first name she had spoken. Even writing about it now makes a wellspring of emotions rise.

Soon after that, I needed to ask Priscilla a very important question. The next day I was supposed to fly to San Francisco for a musicology conference that I had scheduled months in advance. Since this whole incident had sidelined everything, I wasn't sure if Priscilla wanted me to go or stay. Just before I was about to leave, I asked my dad for a little time alone with her. I told her that I loved her and that I wanted to make sure she was okay. I knew her parents were there, but I didn't want to leave her side if she needed me there. I knew that everything I asked had to be in the form of a yes or no question. The conversation went something like this:

"You know I have that conference to go to."

"Yes."

"Would you like me to cancel that and stay with you?"

"No."

"Are you sure?"

"Yes."

"You know I love you, right?"

"Yes."

I kissed her goodbye, and she weakly returned it. I was still scared but knew she was in good hands with her parents and her friends supporting her. I boarded a plane for San Francisco and my first American Musicological Society conference. I stayed with a friend and called Priscilla or texted Nikki or Lisa every day to ask how things were.

At one point, I remember asking Nikki, "Has she let out any swear words?" The text I received in response was something to the effect of, "We've gotten a few fucks and God-damn-its, but that's about it." It was then that I knew, if Priscilla's swearing was coming back, she would be fine.

CHAPTER NINE

Injury and Insult

The recovery process was going to be slow and painful. The bones in Priscilla's legs would need to heal
significantly before she could begin transferring on her
own from the bed to the wheelchair or the toilet to the
wheelchair.

Priscilla came home on November 15 after eleven
days in the hospital. I got back from the musicology conference the day before, and needed a day to get my
affairs in order before I could go see her. Coincidentally,
the day that I saw her was also the day of my birthday.

Priscilla was back at her apartment in Broomfield, but
there had been discussions about admitting her to a rehabilitation facility. I knew what a dreadful decision this was

to make because we had talked about it a month before the accident. That was her worst fear—to go into a home. No one would know how to take care of her, and with her speech reduced to very small words, she wouldn't be able to communicate exactly what she needed.

Instead, Priscilla's parents had been given permission to park their car in the apartment complex lot and stay as long as they were needed to help Priscilla's recovery. The managers at the front office were extremely fond of both Priscilla and me, which helped the situation.

Priscilla was lying in a rented hospital bed, the kind that had the ability to move up and down so as to prevent pressure sores. Unfortunately, this was not ideal for somebody who was brittle and had eight broken bones, because the movement could cause more cracks and breaks.

Priscilla had not expected me to come back after my conference. She told me later that she thought the night of November 7 would be the last time we saw each other. She gave me a birthday present that she had designed before the accident. It included a braille card, a book of recipes, and the children's book *I Love You This Much*. I read it to her only once, while she was lying there in that bed, but I still have all of those things.

I bought pizza for Cledith and Darlene that day to help out because they were still getting used to living there. I only told them later it was my birthday. Buying pizza was the least I could do.

If you have not experienced a stroke or known some-one who has, you might not know that it is imperative that the majority of the hard work of brain recovery is done within the first six months to a year. Otherwise, the neuroplasticity of the brain is not as good, and although the patient will still learn things over time, the chances are best within the first year to get the most function back. This meant that Priscilla was going to have to work hard to recover. Fortunately, from what I was told, the home healthcare program in the state of Colorado was one of the best in the nation. Within a few days after coming home from the hospital, the therapists began arriving. We had a speech therapist, an occupational therapist, and a physical therapist.

The speech therapist, Sue, was a lovely woman with many years' experience. She was habitually forgetful but always confident in her abilities to help patients recover. My knowledge of speech therapy was minimal, so I was interested to see how this would progress.

One of the exercises she started with Priscilla was a call-and-response word repetition game. Sue would say words, and Priscilla would try to repeat them back. The first three or four words were simple, such as ball, cat, chair, and dog. Priscilla knew the words but couldn't get her mouth to say them. Silence followed each of Sue's words. Then, Sue said the word "hand," and in a mono-tone, Priscilla said, "hand." When she realized she had said a word back, she excitedly exclaimed, "HAND!" She raised her left hand in happy recognition that she had made the connection between the word and the thing itself.

This was just one of many such incidents, but I'll never forget the pure joy in her voice when she made that first connection. It didn't register with me until later that that little exercise was the start of a long, but very fulfilling journey of speech, reading, and writing recovery.

The occupational therapist (OT) was less successful in helping Priscilla. Priscilla didn't remember how to do things that she had done automatically. One of these tasks was putting on makeup. I remember her staring into the mirror at the bathroom sink, an eyeshadow in her left hand. The OT was a young girl, and her inexperience with stroke patients was obvious. When Priscilla asked how to put on the makeup, I was not helpful, of course, but neither was the OT, who said, "Well, just do it like you used to do."

That was the problem. How did she do it before? Cognitively, she couldn't remember, and physically, with a loss of sensation on her right side, including her dominant right hand, she couldn't manipulate the applicator. After Priscilla's mother demonstrated it, there was a glint of recognition.

Very gradually, she began to remember how to do things, but she would have to make many adaptations because she couldn't feel the fingertips of her right hand. For example, she could not put earrings on by herself because she used to use tweezers to hold an earring and put the post in her ear, but she didn't have that sort of dexterity anymore. I tried to put them in for her. It was not an easy task for me.

As the Christmas holiday drew near, we all knew that a lot of things were going to be different. However, we didn't expect Priscilla's current roommate, K, to go ape-shit and leave her so soon. We had expected she would fuss about something, as that was her nature, but we didn't expect the chicken to fly the coop with feathers ruffled and flying everywhere.

Priscilla's previous roommate, Teresa, had left to spend the year with friends in Denver. Priscilla's choices for roommates came down to, well, no one, but she wanted to keep the apartment. She went on Craigslist and found a new roommate. (This was before the accident, and during the time I was in New York doing an internship for audio archiving and restoration at the Schenectady Museum of Innovation and Science.)

We'll call the new roommate "K" to make things simple. They interviewed, and it all seemed to go well. K had a little dog, so they figured Katie the guide dog and K's dog Junior could play. When I got back, I met K and things were fine, including the dogs getting along with each other, which was a good thing.

It wasn't long until the ax fell. K's boyfriend dumped her. Normally, I'd use nicer words like "broke up with" or "decided to have a temporary separation with," but no, not this time. From what I heard, it was not a good separation. It didn't take long for Priscilla and I to discover the relationship we shared was a source of K's contempt and jealousy. Things quickly shifted from amicable to hostile, and the table literally turned the other way.

One day, I moved the table so I could sit and do homework. K did not like this, so after I left, she moved it back and treated my moving the table as though it was the sin of all sins. If I recall, she sent angry text messages to Priscilla about the table! It's a fucking table, just move it back and shut up! Yeah … that didn't happen. It only got worse.

Then there was the time that I ate the last of K's multigrain waffles. Priscilla had been used to sharing food with Teresa. They split the groceries and whatever one bought, the other could have if she felt like it. Not with K. She put all the groceries she wanted where Priscilla couldn't reach them. Normally this would make Priscilla angry, but if K wanted to keep separate grocery bills, that was fine with Priscilla.

The waffles were in a place where I could reach them. There were two left, and I didn't think anything of eating them. Apparently, I had crossed into Mama Bear's territory! K sent Priscilla an angry text: "Your boyfriend ate my waffles!!!! Please buy me new ones!" And Priscilla did, if only as a measure to attempt to keep the peace which was rapidly turning into war.

The following weekend, K's boyfriend showed up and they proceeded to show just how "broken up" they were by turning on the music and, well, making noises I DID NOT want to hear. We paid K back in kind later that weekend and walked out of the bedroom feeling pretty satisfied on a few levels. That was the beginning of October, and the chill in the air was a slight wind compared to the chill that hung over the apartment over the coming month.

Finally, the two dogs, Katie and Junior, were separated from playing in the last week before the accident. That was a sad symbol of how fast things were going downhill. K kept her door closed, and the little dog locked inside it. They were whining at each other through the door. It was pitiful, and Priscilla and I exchanged many sighs of disbelief. At that point, we didn't want to do anything that would piss K off even more. You just can't explain to two animals who had had a great time playing in our large living room that they couldn't play together because the humans were having complex relational issues.

But, here's the worst part of it. When Priscilla was still in the hospital, unable to say more than three or four words, K had visited and made a promise. In front of

Priscilla's parents, K promised that she would do all she could to help her recover. She said she would walk with her or cook or do whatever she needed. Priscilla believed her, hoping maybe this would bring them closer together as friends. Maybe the past was the past, and things could be more positive?

After K left Priscilla's hospital room, she said something like, "I'm not sure if I can do this."

Fast-forward to the beginning of December, two weeks before Christmas. K called a meeting with Priscilla and her parents and K's mother. I sat off to the side on the couch and was just there to listen. I'm good at listening.

The gist of the meeting was this: K had given the apartment management a thirty-day notice that she was moving out. She was tired of living in her side of the apartment—with far too much activity on Priscilla's side. She didn't feel like her dog was free to run around the apartment, but Katie was, even though it was at K's discretion to keep her dog locked up. She was tired of me, of Priscilla's parents, and she "just couldn't take it anymore." This gave Priscilla only three choices: find another roommate, move somewhere else, or move back to North Dakota.

I sat there, stunned, hurt, but most of all, I wanted to yell out, "Are you stupid? You signed a lease!!" But I said nothing. As far as I knew, there was no thirty-day notice you could give to break that lease.

Darlene said it best when she replied, "You know, nobody wants to have a stroke."

Priscilla's parents had asked the management office if they could stay to help her recover, and the answer was, "Yes, stay as long as you need," but K claimed she had not been consulted about this.

K and her mother also threatened legal action. This was an absurd thing to do and a scare tactic. They had no grounds on which to sue, but it did scare Priscilla's parents. They were from a small town where lawsuits were not discussed openly—unlike in a big city like Denver where they were thrown around like leaves on a windy day. Naturally, their knee-jerk reaction was of concern. What would they do? Could they pack all of Priscilla's things and move her back to North Dakota? She had a life there.

K proceeded to gather all of her belongings and, after a few hours, left no trace of herself in the house. We never saw her again. We all were shocked at what had just happened.

Priscilla broke down. Then in perfectly clear English, she said, "Well, merry fucking Christmas!"

We laughed at that, and I assured Priscilla we would figure something out, but what? The rent was due in January, and Priscilla could not pay for it all. Could someone really give a thirty-day notice? Could K and her mother really assert legal action when K had signed a lease? I talked to my dad about it.

"Well, Dave, people leave apartment leases all the time," was his response.

It made me think. If one roommate left, could someone else, *like me*, replace her? Yes, the solution was for me to move in. I didn't care much for my living situation at the time anyway. It was a small dorm similar to an efficiency apartment, and I would be much happier with Priscilla at her place, anyway. I also would be saving about $400 a month by moving in with her. So I talked to the head of housing. I explained the situation and was allowed to leave my dorm after the holiday break.

My parents were not happy about this idea. They didn't know that we had discussed moving in together before Priscilla's accident. I had wanted to move more slowly than that, even though I was spending more time at her place than at mine. This roommate situation just added another reason to move forward with our plans. It was a big step that my father was not inclined to accept. As a good father would, he said: "You're just playing the hero to rescue Priscilla from something that you have had no part in. Just think about what you want to do before you do it. What if it doesn't work out between you two?"

He had a point. Once I moved in, especially all the things I had to move, it would be hard to move out again. Could I handle the move and the living arrangements? I told my father, "I don't know, but this is really the only option Priscilla has to avoid going back to North Dakota."

I decided to take the risk. Because my parents were not too happy about it, I didn't ask them to help move my things. Instead, Cledith, Darlene, and I, along with some of Priscilla's friends, moved me and cleaned the place up. Darlene, queen of cleaning, made the place as spotless as she could. The place had been there since about 1948. It was built for vets coming back from WWII to have a place to stay and get their degrees. It likely hadn't been cleaned that well since it was built.

Much like Priscilla's recovery process, my setting up in her apartment happened slowly. I made the previous roommate's room my music and computer room. I got a desk and a dresser, got rid of some things, and bought others. Cledith put things together and took things apart, and we all became a family.

Because Priscilla and I were still in school, we didn't have the required income of two to three times the rent. Thankfully, Priscilla's brother signed the lease to show higher income, and the management of our apartment was not the most skilled at remembering paperwork.

We were in a fragile state in so many ways, but we found a bit of a savior in an outsider who helped us out. A lawyer friend who owned an Italian deli, agreed to take a look at our lease. He said that the claims K and her mother made were preposterous, but that we should change the locks just in case. It took the homeowners association until May to change those locks. We did not rest until they did, still thinking that K might reappear and tell me to get out because she was still on the lease. Who was to say she wouldn't just burst onto the scene again? Despite that, I knew in my heart of hearts that she would never contact us again.

Christmas was a bittersweet affair. I went to my parents' place, and Priscilla and her family went to Lisa's. But from the day after Christmas 2011 until her death on May 25, 2017, Priscilla and I never spent a day apart—a total of 1,977 days.

Chapter Ten

NOLA, Nudity, Dicks, and Shrimp

Nearly a year later and about ninety percent of her faculties recovered, Priscilla, Katie, and I flew into Louis Armstrong New Orleans International Airport. It was Halloween, and I was given a scholarship grant to attend the American Musicological Society conference hosted in the French Quarter. It was the first time I'd been to NOLA, the acronym for New Orleans, Louisiana.

There we discovered New Orleans was the home of jazz, fantastic food, and open displays of nudity, especially frightfully so on Halloween. I was very thankful I was blind. I understood it's an accepted part of the culture, but Priscilla and I were not expecting it. After dropping off our things at the hotel, we arranged for Teresa's friends Jenna and Andy to join us. They were a couple that we had met a few times, and Andy was living in New Orleans completing his med school work. Teresa and Jenna had lived together in Denver after Teresa had moved out of Priscilla's apartment. Jenna was, and still is, a quirky but sweet woman. Andy is quiet and very tall. After figuring out the place where we would meet, Priscilla, Katie, and I set out to find food. We asked the concierge where a good place was, looked in the guide-book as every great tourist does, and started walking. The night was alive with music, cars, and homeless people asking for change.

I knew the history of NOLA from the perspective of music; jazz was like a second language in my mind as far as historical knowledge was concerned. Walking through the French Quarter and hearing live jazz pour out of a few cafes was truly special.

We did not stay at the conference hotel, which was kind of a bummer, but the room blocks had sold by the time we booked. Because I had been to the AMS conference in 2011, I was generally aware of the format. It's pretty simple. People submit hundreds of research papers, and a committee picks the ones they like and puts them into a four-day program. People come from all over the world to hear the presenters share their thoughts and findings. Most of the presenters were American or Canadian, but some came from Europe,

Asia, and Australia. No penguins showed up though, so I guess Antarctica was not represented this time around.

Anyway, staying at a different hotel meant we couldn't hang out with the scholars afterward, not if we wanted to get to bed at a decent time. The conference (and really any well-funded and well-attended conference in any field) ran from 8 a.m. to 8 p.m. or longer.

As was the case with the diverse offering of papers the previous year, this conference had something for everyone, especially all the music nerds who came. Everything was represented, from discussions of tenth-century Italian chant manuscripts to the latest in film music and electronica. There was even a session on music and disability, which we naturally attended.

To make the most of our time, I went to some sessions while Priscilla went to others and recorded them for me. She learned a lot, and I still have those recordings. That's one of the many millions of things I loved about Priscilla: she took in any learning she could. She might not have understood all the music theory behind a Bach organ work or a Miles Davis solo, but she did her best, even after the stroke, to learn as much as she could.

That first night, we decided to go to a very nice restaurant several blocks away on Bourbon Street in the French Quarter. We'll call the restaurant, "The Silver Spoon Fish." We sat down, were given our menus, and reviewed the wine list. That's when our problems began. I was not well-versed in my taste in wine. Neither was Priscilla. When we asked the server what he would recommend, it went something like this:

Dave: What dry wine would you recommend?

Server: Wine is made of grapes. Some are purple. Some are red. Oh, wait, you are blind, so you don't know what I'm talking about.

Dave: Well, I know that there is white wine and red wine, and I don't like the fruity sweet ones like Priscilla does.

Server: Well obviously, this one is sweet and this other one is dry, so just pick something.

This was not going well. Priscilla picked two that the waiter poked toward on the menu, and we moved on to food. I don't remember what I got, except that it was a $35 entrée. That's how unmemorable the food was there, folks. I do remember what Priscilla got, for we told the following anecdote for years to come.

Priscilla ordered a catfish entrée that came with two "gulf rock jumbo prawns." Okay, shrimp, ya gotta have shrimp in a coastal town, right? So, after another round of wine, we waited, and waited, and waited some more. Finally, the food arrived. Priscilla's was apparently a sight to behold, and part of that sight was looking back at her. All I heard was, "Uh, Dave. ..." Then the waiter happened by, and the exchange went something like this:

Priscilla: "Excuse me, sir, um, what are those?"

Server (in a waspish tone): "Those are shrimp, Ma'am." Clearly, he thought she was dumb and a foreigner.

Priscilla: "Right, but, what's that?" She pointed to something on the plate.

Server: "The heads?"

Priscilla: "Yeah! That! They're looking at me!"

Server: "Well, they're born with heads, Ma'am. And eyes that see." I was sure he said that as a jab and meant the shrimp had it better than I did.

Server: "Do you want me to get rid of them?"

Priscilla (in a slightly strangled voice): "Please."

She turned to me, "Dave, they have eyes!" I was laughing so hard I couldn't breathe. She continued, "No, seriously, they were winking at me! Shrimp aren't supposed to do that."

I took a few bites of my food and sips of wine and water to try to get my composure back again. Priscilla, meanwhile, looked like she'd seen a ghost in the form of the crustacean. The waiter returned, and, with the same dismissive manner, said, "Here ya go, Ma'am. Had the chef lop 'em right off for ya," as if lopping shrimp heads off was no different than refilling a glass of water. Priscilla responded with a meek, "Thank you, I appreciate it."

She started eating the rest of her entrée, which she enjoyed. My meal was good, but not great, certainly not

$35 great, but what the hell. I was on vacation, the room and the conference were paid for, and I had some jingle to jangle.

After a bit, Priscilla asked me, "You want these shrimp?"

Hell, yeah I did! Gulf shrimp? To me, they looked like all the other shrimp I'd ever eaten. In this instance, my blindness was a huge asset. I have never seen shrimp with heads on them. I have no intention of ever seeing one. In this case, "seeing" meant feeling them with my hands. Priscilla handed one to me, and after taking a small bite, I asked her why she didn't want them.

"Because I can't get the thought of them winking at me from out of my mind, okay? That was fucking creepy!"

I laughed again. Such were the adventures of the little sheltered girl from North Dakota thrust into coastal culinary waters, confronted by a beady-eyed water bug, grilled, served on a platter, giving her a friendly wink. Two of them.

As I was eating the other shrimp, the waiter came by again and asked how it was. It took all my energy not to start making them talk, which is what I usually did when I had shrimp. Something about using the tail and body as a mouthpiece has always appealed to me.

Priscilla saw what I was about to do and said, sharply, "If you start making those things talk, I will fucking kill you."

Oh, okay, but I was going to make them beg for their lives before I ate them, that's all. No? Okay, fine, I'll be civil in this nice establishment. The wine had kicked in for both of us, more so for Priscilla than me. The giggling had started, and we were well on our way to drunk, but what the hell, why not?

Our waiter, besides being arrogant, talked to Priscilla like she was a child. It's happened before; people see a small female in a wheelchair with an obvious bodily disability and think she's four instead of thirty-four. But this guy did it in a way that really got under our skin. And he wasn't much better when speaking to me. His cultural ignorance was on display, along with a distaste for those of us who were wearing jeans and polos. It was all I had to wear, and I didn't know we were going to be going to a fancy restaurant the first night.

By the time the check arrived, Priscilla was well into her third glass of wine. I, however, was still somewhat sober and not happy with the waiter's treatment of us. Priscilla read me the total, and it was a spendy bill. I told her to put an amount down for the tip. The amount was low, maybe ten percent. Was it a horrible thing to do? Yes, but I had had enough wine that I didn't care what the outcome was at that point; I just wanted to get away from the waiter.

Priscilla wrote down the tip, and the waiter picked up the check. I wanted to see what would happen. I knew he'd look; he was that type. Sure enough, it wasn't twenty seconds later when he came back and said, "Is there anything I could have done better for you guys?" This time, his dismissive tone was replaced by one of clear incredulity that a customer would write whatever amount they wanted.

"Nope. You're fine, thanks," was my dismissive response. We split from that joint like bats outta hell. Then I told Priscilla, "Hey, babe, you realize I only tipped that fucker ten percent, right?"

"It was more than that, I thought. I just wrote what you told me." The wine had worn off a slight bit in the night air.

"Exactly, and I'm glad you didn't question my math skills, because anyone who looks at the tip around the corner and then has the nerve to ask if there's anything he could have done better, needs to just go get a fucking desk job. And the food wasn't even that great, considering the price."

"What should we do?" Priscilla asked as we headed down a sidewalk that clearly needed a lot of TLC.

"Nothing, but never go back and hope that guy learned his lesson."

Now you are probably thinking that I have no soul or conscience. I won't deny that the alcohol flowing through me probably played a part in my decision to give such a horrid tip. However, in my defense, I will say this: When Priscilla and I encountered people who talked to us the way that server did, nine times out of ten, it was in a hospital setting where we had no choice but to put up with the patronizing tone. At the restaurant, it wasn't just the way the server talked, it was his attitude that he was better than we were. He couldn't be bothered to help us pick a wine or a dish and didn't have time for these out-of-towners who had never seen shrimp eyes before. You put those things together, and you get a bad tip. That evening, I didn't have to put up with that tone, and I could teach someone a much-needed lesson. I wonder what happened to that server. He's probably still at the same place, helping out the locals he loves.

Aside from our mishap at "The Silver Spoon Fish," everyone was very friendly and accommodating. We would never forget the amazing experience we had in New Orleans.

CHAPTER ELEVEN

Proposing to a Princess

Before the stroke, Priscilla thankfully had finished all of her journalism classes. Now, nearly a year later, she wanted to give journalism a shot one more time after learning to speak, read, and write again. Journalism was, after all, her passion.

In the fall of 2012, she got an internship with a local news station. She was assigned to transcribe videos. This proved to be an extremely frustrating task for her, and we could not figure out why. She did not tell the people at the news station she had had a stroke because she wanted to see if she could complete the tasks given to her. Unfortunately, the transcription proved to be so anxiety-provoking that she often came home crying.

Anxiety and sensory overload had become new conditions for her, as her brain worked to rewire. She would exclaim to me, "Dave I don't know why I can't do this!"

The answer came from a speech therapist at the University of Colorado, Boulder. Priscilla went there to get extra help because she had used all of her home healthcare speech therapy sessions to recover from the main deficits of the stroke. The therapists ran tests and realized that Priscilla had short-term memory loss. This was the reason she could not transcribe what people were saying. Unfortunately, she had to quit the internship at the local news station, which she deeply regretted. Journalism just was not in the cards for her anymore.

We spent the last two months of 2012 finishing up the incomplete classes that both Priscilla and I had taken for school. An "incomplete" is when you take off the rest of the semester but finish the work later due to an accident or illness, such as we had been through. I had to finish my paper on Franz Liszt for my musicology class, and Priscilla had to finish up her political science degree.

Political science is not an easy subject, even if you haven't had a suddenly acquired cognitive disability, such as a stroke. These were the circumstances that Priscilla was now dealing with: dysfluency (inability to articulate words), dyscalculia (inability to articulate numbers properly), and short-term memory loss. To quote Priscilla, "I had trouble with this shit before the stroke!

How the fuck do they think I'm going to do it now?"

I responded, "What if I helped you to understand it?"

My computer talks to me. That's how I understand what people are writing to me in emails or when I read Facebook. I read things at about 350 words per minute. I was able to read the journal articles for Priscilla's political science class and summarize them for her. It was a definite break from the musicology paper I was finishing up, which was nice. I would read the article, and then, usually using Dragon NaturallySpeaking software, dictate a summary of what I thought the salient points were. We would then sit down and discuss it. I had done some wordsmithing for her during her summer class, but this was the beginning of breaking down things for her so she could understand them.

Oftentimes, people talked too fast for her brain to keep up. She was also a visual learner who somehow ended up with a blind man as her companion. Ironic, isn't it? But we made up for each other's shortcomings. She would describe things to me or read descriptions on coffee packages (I am obsessed with coffee), and I would make things understandable for her if she was struggling to follow a line of dialogue.

She could not have made it through her political science classes without my help summarizing those articles. I don't know if I got the summaries exactly correct, but I know that I at least got close to what the professor wanted. Unfortunately, the professor took an inordinate amount of time to reply to Priscilla's email asking about her grade for the "incomplete." She ended up having to go to the dean of the department and ask him to inquire as to what the grade was.

Priscilla graduated in December 2012 with her double degree in Broadcast News and Political Science. Priscilla's brother, Dion, his wife, Miyako, Miyako's Aunt Riko from Japan, her two nephews, Trent and Cordell, and niece Shantel, and Cledith and Darlene, all came out to see her graduate. It was only one semester later than she had planned. For someone who broke eight bones in her legs and had what could have been a fatal stroke, Priscilla was mighty proud of that graduation.

In true Priscilla Carlson fashion, she had a huge party in January 2013. We bought food from that lawyer friend of ours who owns an Italian deli, and rented a clubhouse at a condo complex to host the event. About sixty-five people came to celebrate Priscilla's achievement.

She would be proud of more than that in the coming year, 2013. Most boyfriends would not have stayed through such a traumatic experience as Priscilla's accident and recovery. I knew, though, that my love for her was more than just a passing fancy. She had my heart long before the accident. What we had been through only cemented those feelings even more. I knew that it was time to make a permanent change to our relationship.

The truth is that after P's stroke, life got real. We had learned that we couldn't take a moment for granted. Nobody knew how long Priscilla was going to live. However, this had been the case from her earliest days after she was born with nine broken bones. I realized that it was time to make our relationship permanent. It was time to propose marriage, but I wasn't going to do it in a way that was traditional because that would be boring. I had to figure out a way to propose that would make a mark.

I thought about doing it on March 18, the day we had our first date. It was also the day when she had moved to Colorado in 2007, but that date didn't mean much to anyone but us, so when else could I do it that would make a splash? How about her birthday?

As with everything I do, putting the plan into action happened quickly. I needed to get the ring, but how was I supposed to do that by myself? I couldn't just go to the jewelry store and pick out any random thing. Coyly, I asked Priscilla what sort of ring she would want. "Vintage princess cut diamond" was her immediate, precise response.

I hadn't a clue what that was, but I knew people who did. I asked my sister, Suriah, and my friend Jon to take me to the mall on a day when Priscilla was busy. We went to three or four stores and I felt like I had an angel on my left and the devil on my right who each thought that different rings would be the best for very different reasons.

The ring would have to be sized for a small finger, but I wanted to give it to her as it was first in case she didn't like it. But how was I supposed to give it to her in a fashionable way without anybody knowing? I had to make sure that Jon didn't say anything. He is my best friend and would be the best man at our wedding, but he had a hard time keeping a secret. Could he keep the secret for three weeks as I prepared my beautifully diabolical scheme? Jon told me later that it was the hardest three weeks he could remember in which he had to keep his mouth shut.

I didn't have a lot of time to prepare for the proposal and presentation of the ring, and there was something else I had to do. On the morning of February 20, 2013, I called Priscilla's parents in Park River, North Dakota. Darlene answered. I asked her what she was doing and was not surprised to hear, "Oh, I've been painting the rental house across the way." It seemed they had been working on that rental house ever since it was built.

"Well, I need to ask you a very important question," I said. Oh boy, how was this going to go? Deep down, I knew the answer, but I also knew that I had to ask out of respect and to be formal about it. There was no getting around it. "I would like to propose marriage to your daughter."

"Absolutely! We think the world of you, Dave, and the fact that you asked really warms my heart. That really means something to me."

We talked a little bit more and then hung up. Okay, got that part done. I had the ring in a box, and I wanted it to be the only birthday gift that she received. How was I going to do that?

Priscilla's birthday was tantamount to Christmas times twenty-eight days. She never had just one birthday; she had a birth month. When I asked her why this was, her response was simple, "The doctors have always said that I could die at pretty much any moment, so when I have a birthday, I've celebrated another year past their predictions."

Luck was in my favor, though. Priscilla wanted to go to the mall to get, of all things, a ring. After her recent graduation from CU Boulder, her brother and sister-in-law had given her some money. She wanted something to commemorate a very hard-fought battle. This was perfect. When we got to the mall, I asked her to drop me off at the makeup counter at Nordstrom department store, so she wouldn't see what I was buying for her birthday. She did this and told the saleslady, "He needs help with picking something for my birthday. Here you go, Dave."

I'm sure the lady at the counter was just as confused as Priscilla was. I remained silent as the sound of Priscilla's electric wheelchair faded away into the noise of the mall as she left to pursue her own shopping goals. Then I explained that I needed to go to the paper store to get an engagement ring wrapped. The woman smiled and guided me down there. I had called ahead of time, so the girl at the paper store knew I was coming with the ring. We had discussed a little plan that involved wrapping paper that was textured, because I love texture. Little did Priscilla know what sort of surprise I had in store for her.

Then we picked up food for the birthday dinner at Lisa's house. We chose Cajun food, which Priscilla had acquired a taste for the previous November in New Orleans. Ironically, the restaurant was not wheelchair accessible, so we parked in the back, and they brought out what looked like a truckload of food.

Keep in mind, nobody knew that I was proposing except Darlene, my sister, and Jon. Throughout the day, Priscilla kept trying to get me to tell her what I was giving her for her birthday. This was a tactic that she employed until her very last birthday. It failed every time, but I knew that she would never forget her thirty-fifth birthday.

The dinner went well, and dessert was imminent. It was beignets. I was so nervous, but I knew when I had to make my move. I was provoked by the line that we quoted for the rest of our married life. Priscilla said with no hint of patience, "Where's my damn gift? Come on, you been hinting about it all day."

I laughed and gave her the most beautiful bag, which contained a box. She began to unwrap the box, but the sparkly paper was so beautiful, she didn't want to tear it. She opened the box with a trembling hand and stopped.

"Um, Dave, there's nothing in here, just tissue paper."

I feigned surprise. "Well, it's there. That's weird. I didn't forget it did I? Just … I know it's there, maybe it's in the tissue paper?"

She and Chris, Lisa's husband, began smoothing out every sheet of tissue paper in the box. Priscilla said, "Nope, nothing there." She was really annoyed.

My response was deadpan. "Ah damn, I forgot to put it in the stupid box. Hold on just a second. I bet it's in my jacket."

I went behind my chair where I had strategically put my jacket so that nobody would mess with the ring's hiding place. Slowly, with everybody watching, I reached into the pocket and pulled out the box. I came around Priscilla's chair and bent down on one knee, just like in the black-and-white movies that we loved so much. I opened up the box, held it in front of Priscilla, and uttered the words I had practiced in my head many times.

"Priscilla, will you marry me?"

There was a general gasp as the ring was displayed,

but Priscilla didn't respond! Nobody had expected this. Moments later, she finally responded with something I had not anticipated.

"Wait! YOU SAID THREE YEARS! I mean … yes, of course!"

By that point, my knees began to fail because I had bad knees thanks to sciatic nerve problems. Unable to stay on one knee for long, I started trembling. I leaned over and kissed her passionately and said *I love you* as cameras flashed.

You may wonder what was so important about waiting three years to marry. It was the length of time that both my brother and my father had waited to propose. It was also the length of time that I had chosen to wait for marriage after we first became serious. That seriousness took on a more life-threatening tone after the accident and stroke, and I had the feeling that I couldn't wait three years. I knew that her response might come a little bit garbled because of the stroke, but I did not expect her sudden outburst to remind me of what I had originally said.

We called her mother and father, and her mother explained that she already knew. The tears had already begun to flow, but telling her live made them flow harder. She wasn't the only one crying. I cried too. Her father made some comment about how he would've said "no," but I can't remember what it was. Typical Cledith sarcasm.

Lisa took pictures and immediately posted them on Facebook. The comments and likes flooded in. My plan had worked! It had probably been the most nerve-wracking moment of my life, but I could finally say that Priscilla was not my girlfriend, she was my fiancé. Within the next fourteen months, she would become my wife.

My sister and Jon enabled me to be a self-advocate to get a ring for my fiancé. I could not have done it without their support and willingness to describe the rings to me. Sure, I felt the rings, but once you've felt a dozen of them, one band feels like another unless there is some tactually defining characteristic about it. The salespeople at the stores were definitely helpful and took their time to explain the rings as well. Sometimes, self-advocacy means reaching out for help to your friends and letting them be your guide through unfamiliar territory. I still never have figured out what a princess cut is. All I know is that I gave one to a Princess.

CHAPTER TWELVE

Blindsided by a Crippling Housing Crisis

In July 2012, we received notice that our rent would be going up a whopping $200 a month. By that time, I was approved to work for Priscilla, thanks to new state programs that paid me to help take care of her medical needs. I made good money, so we could afford the jump in price, still, it was a bitter pill to swallow. Although the rent was doable, we didn't know when or how much it would be raised in the future, so we began focusing on buying our own place.

Priscilla loved that apartment we were renting, and for good reason. It was spacious, and was already set up in a way that worked for both of us. People used to ask us, "Oh, is this a special apartment for people in wheelchairs?" meaning, was it an ADA-compliant space?

We were proud to say, "Nope, just a regular, awesome apartment."

I told Priscilla that we were throwing money down the drain by renting and living there. I even asked the management (a corporation) if we could buy the place. They said no, but it had been worth asking. The big reason to move, aside from equity on a house, was to get a workable garage for the minivan, which was stuck outside in the elements. Although we had a garage, the minivan barely fit inside, and the ramp hit the garage wall, leaving no way for Priscilla to get out. So, there The Enterprise sat outside, no matter the weather.

Starting in the winter of 2012, I got good at scraping the car off when it snowed. Normally, the cold wouldn't be a big deal, but when the temperature dropped to twenty degrees or less, we couldn't go anywhere. The minivan itself would run, but none of the adapted computer systems would work.

We contacted a realtor who had a good reputation and worked in our area. She sat down with us for over two hours and listened to what we needed for accessibility. She seemed to understand what we were going through and how to solve our challenges. However, when she gave us listings of houses, and even some condos, they were almost entirely two-story structures.

This made no sense for us, and our relationship with her did not last long. I ended up dismissing her after her pompous insistence that we would like the place she picked for us. Just because people *think* they understand disabilities, doesn't mean they do.

We combed through listings day after day, looking for places that would work. All of the listings we or the new realtor found went under contract before we could see them. This was common in Colorado at the time. It was called a seller's market.

One house that was available was a dreadful one located next to our apartment complex. It was built in 1956. It was a test case to see how our new realtor and my parents would react to it. We pulled up to find the realtor and my dad walking out of the home, locking the door. We were stunned, why would they do that?

They approached our car and said, "It has stairs. You'll never get your ramp up there to get in."

Well, this was the absolute WRONG thing to tell Priscilla Carlson. See, Priscilla had been born with the idea that, if she didn't try something herself, and someone said she couldn't do it, then she *had* to try it herself. It was a rebellious streak that carried her through an inaccessible high school, college problems, and even her stroke and recovery. It's how she was.

Priscilla was furious that they would, literally, close the door on this opportunity for us as home buyers.

I said, "Well, that's that, I guess."

To which she responded, "The hell it is. We're gonna try and get in there if it kills us."

There was no arguing with that statement. We told Dad and the realtor that we wanted to try, so they pulled out the ramp, and we got out of the car. Now, picture this scene: It's a rundown neighborhood/construction area, a rundown house, and it had snowed heavily a few days before. But we were determined. Priscilla and I trudged through the landscaping of rocks and snow; I had to push her through it, and that chair weighed 240 pounds plus her weight.

I clearly remember the astonishment in the realtor's voice as he watched us from behind. "Wow, you guys make a pretty good team. I'm impressed."

We just smiled. Priscilla went up the ramp into the dingy little house, and we were in. My mother came in with us and asked if Priscilla's chair could fit in the laundry room.

"I don't think it will," was Priscilla's quiet response.

Happily, her chair fit through the doorway (just barely), and she could turn around three times in the space of the room. Her response was a raised fist and the word, "BAM!!!" This was one of her favorite exclamatory words.

Just to add icing on the cake of "Priscilla and Dave can actually get into this house," we left the parents alone for just a minute, and just to see what they would do, we did something really bold.

Priscilla said in a loud voice, "Yeah, Dave, I think we should make an offer on this house. I like it. It's close to where we live already, and the area isn't too bad."

That was far from the truth. The surroundings consisted of a portable toilet on one side of the house, standing for all to view, and a construction site on the other side. We had no idea what the construction was for, but it looked like a low-rent housing project.

My parents were floored. "You what?!"

We left the house saying we'd think and talk about it a little more. We never told them it was a test. From that day onward, I'm pretty sure my parents let Priscilla do whatever she wanted, knowing that we would be a team and figure out how to do it.

Eventually, we found a listing for a condo that was still being built. It was about three miles away and still in Broomfield where we lived. We went there and talked with the management company and decided, after looking at the floor plan and the location of the bus stop, that we wanted to live there. The price range worked for us, and they were building with luxury materials. The condos would be done by the end of the summer. Perfect, just enough time to get my master's thesis written, graduate, get a mortgage, and move into a beautiful new home.

We were so excited that we didn't really consider all of the terms in the contract. This was my fault because I was responsible for reading it over. We signed the contract on March 20, a fateful day for three reasons. First, the contract was signed. Second, we hired our new housekeeper, and third, the shower door spontaneously exploded because of a micro crack that had been building pressure within the glass. The door was in thousands of diamond pieces on the floor of the bathroom. It was a sight to behold, and the noise alone scared us beyond belief. Later, Priscilla and I would consider that explosion an omen of the events about to unfold.

Other problems arose, starting on the day that we signed that contract. The builder was not expecting us to request automatic door buttons on each of the doors to get into the building. We had assumed these would be installed because it was a condo. We later sent the building representative links to several websites that offered automatic doors and pricing, but we had a suspicion that they ignored our email. Over the next several months, I was responsible for convincing these people that they needed to pay the money to install the buttons. Unfortunately, they were under no legal obligation to do so because they had billed themselves as a residence instead of a commercial property. According to the Americans with Disabilities Act, private residences were not required to be built with modifiers such as automatic doors. Our hands were tied.

I have dealt with some very defensive people in my life, but no one was more defensive and aggressive than the builder of these condos. You could have told this man that the sky was blue, and he would immediately begin arguing with all of his might that it was green. He and I spent several hours going back and forth on why these doors were important. I eventually got him to understand, but it was like pulling shark's teeth. The builders then made a ramp so that Priscilla could go in and see the unit; we thought this was a step in the right direction toward restoring the peace between us and the builder.

Our unit was one of the first to be constructed because it was on the main floor. We installed beautiful hardwood floors and a fireplace. The area seemed spacious and included a workout facility at the end of the hall. The floors were still being built as we toured our section. We walked to the bus stop and back during the daytime and figured that it wasn't so bad. Sure, it was about a mile, but it was a small price to pay for the luxury we had in this beautiful place. It would soon be ours!

There was just one problem besides the doors—the mortgage. Anybody who has bought a house knows the hassle and difficulty of getting papers ready for the signing away of your life, aka a thirty-year mortgage. In our case, it was after the 2008 recession, and mortgages included more regulations than in the past. On the plus side, interest rates were at historic low points. We never met our lender in person, which I thought was strange. Instead, we emailed documents back and forth, including tax returns and statements of disability. We locked in a good rate and had most of the necessary documentation.

The only problem was that our debt-to-income ratio was too large. Anybody who has ever had to deal with this sort of thing knows what a pain it is to figure out how much you can or can't spend to lower this ratio. I won't go into all the specific statistics, but it was a grueling process, and I was writing my master's thesis at the time. It is still exhausting to think of all the exchanges and documents and headaches necessary to qualify for a place that hadn't been built yet.

I looked at several other lenders, including credit unions, but all of them basically told us the same thing. Rates were the same across the board, and documentation and qualification were still dependent on financial things we were trying to change.

We ended up backing out of the condo contract, which cost us some money, but not as much as we had originally put down. The builder did not complete the construction on time (which didn't surprise anyone), and the loan was a disaster. We also had to get a lawyer to threaten legal action. Our realtor had signed on one page that he was representing us, and on the facing page that he was representing the builder and management agency. That kind of behavior is either illegal or highly unethical. Either way, we did not work with that realtor again. We learned a lot from this dreadful experience. Most importantly, we learned not to be as impulsive as we had been, to dot our i's and cross our t's when signing contracts, and to know who we were dealing with.

Our third, and last, realtor helped us buy the home we settled in. We met her when we were fed up with the condo-buying process. We picked a random house that was cute, but we knew we were never going to buy it. We just wanted to meet the realtor and see if it was marginally accessible. It had been built in the '50s, so the chances were slim.

This realtor, Suddha, was so understanding and had a Zen-like quality that was a breath of fresh air after our previous realtor. After debating about what to do, we told her that we were still under contract with this other jerk of a realtor, but that we were getting out of it. We asked if she would be willing to start looking at things when we were ready, and she agreed. Three months later, she began sending us new listings without any pressure to buy.

Fast-forward to May of 2014. Priscilla had a lot of work to do for the Statewide Independent Council, for which she worked as a coordinator. Suddha had been in India helping her mother who had knee surgery.

However, she was still dutifully sending us listings when she saw places that might work. On May 6, she sent us a listing that looked too good to be true. It was a 2005 condo with a five-piece bath, a nearby bus stop, and a host of other features that screamed accessible.

Priscilla was reluctant to go. She had a lot of work to do and felt like she was getting sick. We had also just finished writing and acting in a play for Phamaly Theatre Company, a theater group made up of people with disabilities. Oh yeah, the wedding was a month and a half away.

I looked at the list we had compiled of things we would need to have in order to make a home accessible for us both. Some were features we had to have, while others would have been nice, but the condo could work for us without them. This new listing had nine of ten items on that list, so I told Priscilla that we had to see it. Suddha's representative, Ilsa, met us at the place, six miles from where we lived.

It was love at first sight! We walked around the building to find a fountain dripping quietly while classical music played from speakers. Immediately, I began analyzing from which period of music history the piece came, what key it was in, and …

"Dave! We're here for the house, not the fuckin' music!" Priscilla said.

Right.

Just then, Ilsa arrived. Of pure Austrian stock, complete with accent, she radiated confidence and sass as only the Austrians can. We went upstairs through the secure entrance (the condo was on the second floor), and we loved the place. The walls were white, but they could be painted. The place was big enough and had recently been vacated and put on the market. The best part was that there was *heated, underground parking.* This meant that The Enterprise wouldn't have to sit out in the elements, and the computers wouldn't freeze! If you've ever dealt with computers, you know that there are optimal temperatures for them to operate, so they don't overheat or get too cold to function. In the case of the computers that ran the car, we discovered that they would not function if they had been outside and the temperature was 20 degrees Fahrenheit or lower. That was something we found by trial and error. Yet another reason for us to have a parking garage was to avoid the possibility of an accident with ice at the end of the ramp that Priscilla used to get in and out of the car.

We made an offer that night and woke the next morning to a counter offer. Oy. This was not going to be easy. What was easy this time, thankfully, was getting the documentation together for the loan because we had been through the process before. This, as Priscilla made clear, was my job. She was too busy with work and didn't want to deal with the numbers and the pain of the last debacle.

"Just tell me what you need from me, and I'll give it to you," she had said flatly.

That was easy enough, but how could we make our offer better than the other bidder's offer? We had an escalation clause at least, which said something to the effect of: "If the other offer is X amount of dollars, we will pay Y amount of dollars more to get this property." It seemed a bit shaky, but that's all we had, or was it?

The lender agreed to meet in person on Sunday. Remember what I said earlier about meeting your lender in person? Yep, got that out of the way right away. Anyway, we were talking, and she made a suggestion I had to ponder. What if I wrote a letter to the seller of the home, explaining our "situation"? It wasn't as if we could just go buy a home because it was there. This one met all of the requirements we needed for a home. I asked Ilsa, and she agreed to the plan.

I needed to get the letter done quickly. I couldn't sleep the next morning, so I started writing. And then I wrote some more. And some more. Pretty soon I had a substantial document. I liked to write essays that I think people will like to read, but the reality was that these people were probably busy and just wanted to sell the condo.

After finishing a draft, I edited it, then edited again, and again, and the realtor was almost shouting at me to get the thing done before it was too late to submit it to the sellers. Priscilla was frustrated too. She knew how much of a perfectionist I am, but this was our one shot—our one chance to get our dream home! I sent the letter to Ilsa at 3:58 p.m.—with two minutes left to spare before the deadline. Meanwhile, just in case, I had to have all our documents ready for the loan, so I gathered those up.

We waited.

And waited.

And waited some more.

We were told that we would have a decision by Friday morning. Those two days felt like two years. We sat in the apartment, hardly daring to breathe, looking at Priscilla's phone every time it vibrated. More often than not, it was a Twitter notification or news story. Finally, at 11:40 a.m. on May 10, we received word that we had gotten the condo!

We were both relieved beyond belief. Apparently, the letter I wrote made all the difference. The other party had made the same offer as far as a price was concerned, and they had a higher escalation clause than we did, but because of the letter I wrote, the seller picked us.

The next few weeks were full for us. Between Priscilla's work and my figuring out the mortgage, it was a busy time. And oh yeah, the wedding, we had that to plan too.

Then the lending company asked the stupid question, "How long will Priscilla's disability last?"

Why this was asked, I have no idea. After all, the lender herself spent two or more hours with us going over documents in person. It wasn't as if Priscilla was going to get super strong and grow to be five feet tall! We felt this was going too far. It's one thing to ask what the disability is, it's another to doubt whether it is an actual disability that just might disappear.

From the lending company's perspective, they probably wanted to make sure they were not getting swindled, but I had had enough. Rarely do I use this word, but I found their behavior to be bordering on, if not outright, discrimination, and I sent them an email saying so. That did the trick; we got the loan the next day.

Buying a home is stressful for anybody. The first realtor that we worked with gave us every indication that she knew about disability and accommodation, but clearly didn't want the responsibility of looking at homes that would cater to our needs. The second realtor showed us some properties which included the condo that we almost bought. The people in that fiasco were really only concerned with the bottom line, which would explain some of the defensive behavior we encountered. Luckily, the third realtor completely understood what we were going through and what we needed to find in a home. The fact that she sent us local listings while caring for her ailing mother in India should tell you enough about her work ethic and her hope for us to find a place to live. You have to know when self-advocacy can get you into bad situations in order to know when the good ones come up.

Chapter Thirteen

A Timeless Vintage Wedding

Priscilla and I knew that we wanted a wedding that reflected both of our interests and personal tastes. Work began almost immediately after I proposed to figure out the venue and what time of the year we wanted to get married. We had originally wanted a fall wedding, but that meant that harvest would be going on in North Dakota. Harvest was when Priscilla's parents could make money working to unload trucks of potatoes, sugar beets, and other crops. They did not own a farm themselves, but the entire town and the surrounding ones were all agriculturally driven. Harvest in the fall and planting in the spring were the big times for that area. We decided that late June would probably be best.

One thing I wanted to immediately make clear with any wedding planner or venue was that our wedding was not just the bride's day. It was my day too. This was something I had seen time and time again. I asked Priscilla why it's usually all about the bride, and the groom just sort of shows up. Her response was, "Because he usually doesn't give a shit and just shows up and does what he's told."

It made me extremely angry to be put in such a submissive role, so I decided to dispel the idea. I had Priscilla's full support on this because she believed it too and knew how headstrong I was. The first venue we went to implied almost immediately that the wedding was "her day." I jumped in vehemently saying that I was actually the one who was researching the wedding venues, and that I was just as much a part of the event as anybody. The planner was taken aback by my forwardness, but that's what I wanted to happen.

Another thing we experienced was a certain patronization that occurred at a few of the venues we visited, where the staff talked to us as if we didn't know what a wedding was. To them, we were "That cute couple. He helps her in the wheelchair, and she helps him see." It was surely a subconscious thought for some people, but others made their thoughts obvious, which immediately left a bad taste in our mouths. While this attitude was nothing new to us (it happens often in hospitals), it seemed as if some people were absolutely amazed that we were getting married at all because we had disabilities. Again, their reactions were probably subconscious, but they often spoke to us with a certain vocal inflection, as if they were talking to children.

We decided not to go with a wedding planner. This was a decision that we made almost immediately after seeing Priscilla's cousin's wedding get royally fucked up. I won't go into detail about that, but let's just say that the main cake was not the right cake and that was only the beginning of it.

We looked for a hotel that would accommodate all types of disabilities, so we could be as independent as possible. The first hotels we visited did not appeal to us. One of them had dreadful food and was very expensive. The other had a manager who was strange and made us feel uncomfortable. Finally, we settled on a hotel in downtown Denver.

I didn't think we could afford it, but we decided to take a chance. We met the woman, whom I will call Sally, in charge of preparation and planning. She was not a specific wedding planner, but she worked for the hotel, organizing event catering, decorations, setup and teardown, etc. We immediately felt a great vibe from her. She treated us like human beings who were getting married and who also happened to be blind and in a wheelchair. Sally and I had spoken on the phone a few times because I was the one doing the venue research. She knew that I was not going to just let it be the "bride's day."

Priscilla and I decided to have a vintage wedding. We wanted to invoke the classic films and music of the 1940s and '50s, which we had met and bonded over in 2011. The ambiance of the hotel catered to our vintage idea because it had a lot of kitsch, and each floor had a theme to it. Vintage posters and pictures hung on the walls everywhere. And, did I mention, it was cheaper than the other one we considered?

Picking the bridal party and groomsmen was a simple process; we knew how many people we needed to have, and we asked them formally. Jon was the best man, that was a given. Priscilla's cousin Michelle was maid of honor because Priscilla had been maid of honor at her wedding.

Some of the hotels we visited told us that we could sample their menu by going into the restaurant for dinner. The hotel that we picked did things differently by buying us dinner at their restaurant so that we could taste some of the food, or at least their chef's typical style. For the wedding tasting itself, we had little menus and went through them with friends and family to try and decide what people would eat.

My family has always had eclectic taste and experimented in the culinary field (my mother taught herself to be a gourmet cook). Priscilla's family, on the other hand, enjoyed a North Dakota meat-and-potatoes diet and would not be necessarily keen on all the entrées that were listed on the menu. I do recall a few long nights trying to figure out what exactly her mother and grand-mother would eat. We finally settled on the things that we wanted to taste and went to the hotel dining room and sampled all of the dishes. They were divine. There was just one small detail left—the cake!

I told Priscilla shortly after I proposed that if I was to have a wedding cake, I would love it to have a baseball theme. I had always been obsessed with baseball, and my obsession had grown more intense after the 2007 World Series in which the Rockies were sadly swept by the Red Sox. I tried not to miss a game and had told Priscilla shortly after we started dating that if I didn't an-swer a text or call, I was most likely watching a game. Baseball is almost like a religious experience for me be-cause it's a sport that I can visualize as it happens, unlike basketball or football, in which too many things happen at once for me to get a good mental picture.

So, we agreed that we would have a baseball cake. Sally was enthusiastic about the idea, if not a little ner-vous. On the day that we went to taste the five different types of cakes we had picked, the bakery chef, Kelly, came up from the kitchen to meet us. She was a spright-ly little thing who seemed to have boundless amounts of energy.

Kelly presented us with a hand-drawn sketch of her vision of the baseball-themed cake. It was far more elaborate than we had planned, but it was perfect. We had pictured a cake with a baseball theme on the top. Kelly made an entire cake that looked like a baseball, complete with stitching on the frosted sides. It was hard for me to visualize, but I got an idea of what it looked like based on people's descriptions. I still have that drawing in our wedding memorabilia box.

For the layers, we chose a chocolate coconut layer, a dark chocolate layer, and a chocolate peanut butter layer. Those were difficult decisions, but it was an absolutely fun tasting experience. You wouldn't think that deciding which type of cake tasted better would be a difficult process, but that's how good this cake was! It was, however, easier than choosing the dinner, the invitation design, and the save-the-date cards.

We wanted our music to be different from the usual overplayed wedding songs, and we wanted our first dance to make an impression. For the record, I don't like to dance. It makes me feel awkward because I can't see what other people are doing. Even though most everyone on a dance floor is into themselves, it's still a strange feeling for me. Our first dance was going to be just Priscilla and I, with our closest friends and family watching. We wondered how we could choreograph something that would make people take notice. Then we thought of the people we knew who were in a wheel-chair dance company in downtown Denver. Some of them were also part of our theater group, Phamaly.

We approached the founder of the dance company, and she agreed to help us with our first dance. Surprisingly, the song choice was easy, *Devoted To You* by the Everly Brothers. It was slow enough to shuffle to, with a beautiful melodic line and those tight harmonies that only the Everly Brothers could pull off. I took the guitar intro (which has that twangy little vibrato that was so common to 1959) and looped it three or four times to give Priscilla and I enough time to make our entrance. And what an entrance it was! The coolest fifteen seconds of my life!

Normally, it was a cardinal sin to stand on or otherwise put one's feet anywhere on Priscilla's wheelchair. She once ran over a teacher who did that after asking him to stop and giving him enough warnings. But for our wedding dance, I was permitted to stand on the back of her chair as she and I entered the dance floor. We did this for a few reasons. First, we wanted to make an entrance that wasn't just me holding onto her chair the way I usually did. Second, we wanted to see what her mother would say.

Darlene was very particular about not ruining the paint on things, especially Priscilla's chairs. So, we figured that if I stood on the back of the chair, my shoes might rub the paint on the plastic base of the chair. We pictured Darlene's horrified face and could almost hear her immediate thought, "Oh shit, I hope he doesn't ruin the paint!"

We were both nervous about this little stunt because if I fell, I could break an ankle. Fortunately, I had great balance, and we went slowly enough. We had also practiced it a lot, just to make sure Priscilla was okay with my extra weight. I asked if we could make this our preferred mode of regular transport, but she didn't go for the idea. In fact, I think her specific retort was, "No! Because then you will actually ruin the paint on my chair, and I'll have to kill you."

Eh, can't blame a guy for tryin'.

We made a few glorious revolutions around the floor before we started the main dance. The dance itself was a series of circles, promenades, and showoffs of both bride and groom. We knew the exact dimensions of the dance floor, and we had worked with our choreographer to move within those limits. Over the space of four rehearsals, we assembled the dance.

The dance company never charged us for their help, but we gave them a generous donation after the wedding was over.

Society has strange ideas about weddings. A number of times, I was told it was the "bride's day." I was not having any of that! Self-advocate Dave reared his well-groomed head and said, with a flourish, "I will not stand for this treatment!" It was the groom's day as well. Throughout the entire wedding-planning process, we found a number of people both willing and not willing to understand our disabilities. Some took the sappy view that we found condescending, "Oh how sweet! The disabled people are getting married!" I don't think they even knew that this was offensive or condescending, it's just how they were. Those people were in the minority.

The people at the hotel we ended up choosing understood that we needed to make accommodations for both blind people and people in wheelchairs, but they were more than happy to do it, which made us feel extremely proud that we chose that spot for our wedding. Yet another example of how being a self-advocate means that you have to speak up for what you want and what you truly believe is right.

Chapter Fourteen

Priscilla's Comeback

One of the ways in which we both furthered the advocacy cause was to participate in two plays by the Phamaly Theatre Project. This is a theater company based in Denver comprised of actors and actresses with disabilities. These particular plays were called *Dislabeled*. Priscilla participated in the second and third manifestations of these comedies. I participated in the third one.

The first one that Priscilla participated in was in 2013 and was a series of sketches which loosely revolved around a director (the man who actually directed the troupe and wrote the script) and his complete ignorance of people with disabilities. Priscilla's run-in with him involved the mispronunciation of her name. This was an extremely common occurrence in our daily lives because of the sound of her voice. Our personal favorite incident was when someone thought her name was Crisbulla, which reminded us of the cereal Crispix. The director in the play called her Miscella, Ercela, and Patricia. Patricia was often what people called her since Priscilla was not a common name, after all.

The play in which I participated was a courtroom drama/comedy. The premise a group of protesters fighting segregation of people with disabilities. They wanted people with intellectual/cognitive disabilities to live within the community rather than be institutionalized. Somehow, the protesters—of which I was one—managed to burn down the nursing home that they were picketing. You would probably think that because of her obvious disability, Priscilla would be the defense attorney. Instead, she was the prosecuting attorney who was ready to throw the book at the "unruly hooligans."

During my testimony, she was particularly vicious and gave me several ice-cold stares and eye rolls, which I thankfully couldn't see. I was playing a blind person in the play, so I didn't have to act too out of character. While there was plenty of drama in the story, there was also a very keen sense of comedic relief. One of these moments came during my testimony when I complained about giving my oath on the Bible presented in front of me. One of my lines was, "Hey, there's no braille on this thing. I could be swearing on a book of carpet samples, for all I know."

I took the oath and, after a brief exchange between attorneys, the judge, and myself—in which I informed everybody that my archery class had been canceled on the day of the protest and that I had been trying to buy a *Playboy* before the demonstration took place—the judge asked me this question which always got a huge laugh from the audience:

Judge: "Just curious, is there porn for the blind?"

Me: "Yeah, but it's not so great. It's just two dots and a triangle."

On November 4–6, 2016, the inaugural Self-Advocacy Summit was held in Colorado Springs. This was a three-day retreat comprised of speakers and panels about different types of self-advocacy for people with primarily intellectual disabilities. It was sponsored by the Developmental Disabilities Council of Colorado. The summit showed people with intellectual disabilities how they could communicate and interact with the world around them.

Priscilla organized the summit over a period of about six months. It was stressful for her to organize a massive event like this. Over one hundred people registered, and every session was filled to capacity, but it represented the culmination of everything she had worked for since her accident in 2011. Priscilla had always been a self-advocate for people in wheelchairs, but after she had her stroke, she realized the things that she was missing and had more difficulty with, like speaking, writing, reading, and cognition. As she put it, "I know what it's like not to have a voice, to have things that you took for granted taken away from you, and not be able to communicate."

Perhaps by coincidence, a stroke of fate, or just sheer luck, the dates of the summit coincided with the dates of Priscilla's accident and stroke in 2011. This was something that I don't think she had thought about, but I did. I arranged for the people who were helping with the organization of the conference to purchase a bouquet of flowers to present Priscilla on the last day. Originally, I was going to give her the flowers as a token of everybody's appreciation for all the things that she had done. I decided to take things one step further.

I chose to sing "Rise Up" by Andra Day at the end of the conference. It's a song of hope in which the singer tells somebody (her lover, a friend, we're not really sure) that she will be a source of strength in downtimes, and lift his or her spirits so he or she can soar to the heavens. I learned the song by listening to it several times and practicing it while packing up our hotel room that morning.

When I presented Priscilla with the flowers, I took the microphone, and said, "It has been five years since

Priscilla fell out of her chair, broke eight bones in her legs, and had a massive stroke on her left side. Today, she has managed to organize a very successful conference, showing the world that she can come back from something that could have been her undoing. Instead of completely giving up and not doing anything about her predicament, she fought with all of her physical and mental strength to restore her communication, dignity, and pride."

I then sang the song, thanked everybody, and the conference came to a close. It made a big impression and was a catharsis for everybody there; we had come far within one weekend to understand that the world was not always full of doom and gloom, and there were always alternatives to problems that had previously seemed insurmountable.

CHAPTER FIFTEEN

DePraved

The six months between the Self-Advocacy Summit and our next trip to North Dakota were filled with a mixture of good and bad for Priscilla and me.

We went to Washington, D.C., to present a poster at the Association of University Centers on Disabilities (AUCD) conference, which was well-attended. We also worked on our coaching based on classes we attended at the Coaches Training Institute, and these classes were truly life-changing for both of us. In January of 2017, we stepped in to fill a self-advocate position at JFK Partners. This organization is affiliated with the American University Centers for Developmental Disabilities. It was the same role that Priscilla helped start the previous

August. In addition, on April 1, 2017, she started a part-time position with the University of Colorado Anschutz Medical Campus doing their social media dissemination. In other words, Priscilla was the one who would post social media updates about the goings-on at JFK Partners, keep up the mailing list, promote events on social media, and so forth.

We were busy, but on the health front, things were not looking good for Priscilla. Let's back up a bit. Around Thanksgiving of 2014, Priscilla broke her left arm. It had been hurting for about two months because she had to lean on the front of the bathroom counter when she used the sink, which put pressure on the bone. I woke up to a scream of pain and immediately got painkillers and thus began a year-long saga of what to do with the broken left radius and eventually cracked ulna. Without going into the literally painful details, doctors tried four different casts and/or braces with four different variations on each, making a total of sixteen combinations. The doctor who helped us with this worked as a trauma surgeon for both Denver's University Hospital and Children's Hospital.

Priscilla was, in essence, a liability. She was too old to be seen by the only doctor in the area familiar with OI, but needed some sort of medical care for the broken arm. It would have been very, very risky to do surgery because Priscilla's arm was so small, and the rod from childhood was still holding it in place. Her right arm, which had had one of the rods pop out when she was six years old, developed without a humerus, the bone in the upper arm. We always said that it was a very "serious" arm. It made sense that Priscilla was never strong in that arm and, due to the fact that there seemed to be only a fragment of the humerus, she could wave at people behind her back. It was a great party trick that you either found disgusting or funny in a twisted sort of way. If you don't laugh at a situation you can't do anything about, then where is the fun in life?

The doctor, Doctor S., was not an easy person to work with and was thoroughly confounded by the fact that somehow Priscilla could move her left arm, despite the cracked and broken bones that showed up on the X-rays. He was the best hope we had, considering Priscilla's age and the fact that Children's Hospital would not let her in because of the stroke which happened under their care. The last comment Doctor S. made to us in our last appointment was characteristic of his demeanor, "Well, I guess I'll see you when I see you …"

Her left arm was as stable as it could be. I had to help with some of Priscilla's daily living needs, but I don't regret a second of that time. Even though breaking her arm was painful and led to less mobility on the left side, Priscilla was able to be a self-advocate and tell other people about things she had learned when needing to modify her daily living activities, such as showering. We both discovered a lot about new devices that were on the market, and we had to be creative with how we did things. Our rallying cry became, "Okay. How're we gonna do this?"

That last year was a struggle. Priscilla developed kidney stones that were most likely caused by an experimental drug originally prescribed to patients with osteoporosis. She was prescribed the drug to strengthen her bones. The downside was that it created excess calcium, which her body did not know what to do with. Upon reaching the two-year mark of her taking the drug, we discussed the options with the doctor who was at the Center for Bone Research in Lakewood, Colorado. If Priscilla continued to take the drug, her bones would be stronger. The risk was that there would still be kidney stones to deal with.

Priscilla decided to continue taking the drug and to take the risk because, as she said, "If I take the drug, my bones get stronger, and I feel like they are the strongest they have ever been. If I don't, my bones become frail and I'm really tired of dealing with cracking and breaking bones because I've dealt with it all my life."

I told her that I would support her in any decision that she made and would continue to give her the drug which was administered by a shot in her leg from a syringe.

We were not without our humor during these times. When the doctors discovered a three-millimeter kidney stone in her left kidney, we decided to name it Rocky. I originally thought it was in reference to the flying squirrel of Rocky and Bullwinkle fame. She corrected me and said that it was in reference to the *Rocky* movies starring Sylvester Stallone. "I want to fight the Motherfucker just like Rocky. It's goin' down!" said Priscilla.

We never did manage to find the stone, but she did pass it. The doctors were concerned that they were going to have to perform surgery to get the first Rocky out, but she managed to pass that one. That was a blessing because no one knew exactly how the surgery would be done, and it might require two teams of doctors, one for a pediatric body, another for an adult body. Keep in mind, Priscilla's organs were all adult-sized, but compacted into a thirty-four-inch frame. Because of this, the doctors weren't even sure where her kidneys were located at times.

We named subsequent kidney stones Rocky II, followed by Apollo Creed and, finally, Mr. T.

Priscilla was also being seen for sinus issues at this time. She had always had sinus issues, especially in humid North Dakota. But now, she felt like she had cement in her nose. I was helping her use an inhaler more and more. We were still doing the self-advocacy project, and she was working the checkout at Walgreens (a nice break from disability-related things). In addition, her social media job with the University of Colorado had begun after they finally figured out the funding.

A break was just what we needed in May of 2017. It had been a trying year for us. In the previous two months, I could not have counted the number of doctors we were seeing to figure out what was going on with Priscilla's kidney stones.

Despite this, the most important thing for Priscilla at that time was to see her nephew Trent graduate from high school, and attend one of his baseball games. Her brother's eldest had graduated two years earlier, and now it was Trent's turn. But the Priscilla who stepped onto the plane to North Dakota was tired, worn down, and having constant headaches. Something was not right. Maybe it was just too much stress. We needed this vacation. Then we could come back and reassess the situation.

When Trent's high school baseball game was over, Priscilla and Cledith were walking back to the car. Darlene and I had been sitting around, just figuring they were socializing with family. All of a sudden, Priscilla stopped and exclaimed, "Dad, I got a headache. Get me in, Dad."

"What's that, sweetheart?"

"Get me in, quick."

They lowered the minivan ramp as they had done so many hundreds of thousands of times before. Priscilla wheeled into the van, and I went around to the other side. By the time the door opened, she had started seizing. She was making a noise that I had never heard before. I knew all of the sounds in her "symphony of sounds," but this was like a new instrument that was not welcome in the present score. It was a snort. That's the best way I could describe it.

Her mother exclaimed that Priscilla was convulsing and foaming at the mouth. "Should we get her to the hospital?"

"Yeah! I guess so!" I said. "Priscilla, Sweetheart! Can you hear me!?"

The noise was unrelenting. Darlene kicked the engine into gear, and we moved as fast as we could across the field, the baseball diamond behind us. She still wasn't responding.

"Sweetheart, if you can hear me, can you squeeze my hand?" I don't know if it was luck or if she had heard me, but she clenched my hand. It was not the loving hand-holding we had done thousands of times since our first date. It was a death grip.

"Okay, now, can you let go of my hand?"

She did and opened her eyes. "Huh?" she said softly.

"We have to take you to the hospital, Sweetheart," I said trembling.

"Why?" Her barely audible response sounded as if she had just woken from a nap and still thought that it was night when it was day.

"Because you're sick. Something's wrong," I said.

She began to seize again. By this time, we had arrived at the hospital. There are advantages to living in small towns. One of them is that the hospital is not miles and miles away through vast swarms of unforgiving traffic.

Then I noticed something different. I felt her leg and smelled urine. Priscilla had lost control of her bladder. This was bad. This was very bad because that was the last thing Priscilla would do consciously.

We were all panicking, and I couldn't figure out where the God-damned lever was to unlock her wheelchair. Darlene was yelling at me to get it unlocked. How many thousands of times had I unlocked that chair without a thought, and this one time, I couldn't figure out where it was! I finally found it. It had seemed like an eternity to try and find it. I jumped out, and Cledith backed the wheelchair, slowly, oh so slowly, out of the car while the woman behind us was asking if we could move our car.

"Well, we kind of have an emergency here," Darlene said, and she was clearly just as shocked as I was at the woman's comment.

Priscilla was still making a horrific noise when they wheeled her in. I told the nurse I had been with Priscilla at every major doctor's appointment since 2012.

We got her up on the table, and she was soaked in urine. I had yelled for them to get her on oxygen. I was in full command form because I was used to people who had not dealt with *osteogenesis imperfecta* and had forgotten that this doctor had seen Priscilla before. Nevertheless, I started rattling off the usual, "She's brittle, be careful if you use a blood pressure cuff …"

At one point, I grabbed her phone and pulled out her list of medications. I handed them to the nurse who thankfully knew how to use an iPhone.

They did a CT scan of her head. It showed blood on the brain. Then her heart stopped. The doctor came in and said they were going to have to put a tube down her throat, so she could breathe. I begged them not to do it because the last person I knew who had had that done could hardly speak. That was the last thing that Priscilla needed. My pleading was met with the simple response of: "If we don't, she will die."

There was no arguing with that statement. They had to do CPR and broke several ribs in the process. When her mother inquired as to why that had to be done, the doctor responded with, "Ribs can heal, hearts can't." I liked this doctor. I had heard about him. He was efficient.

Meanwhile, Priscilla's father stayed in the waiting room with me. "Dave, I just came from this place last week," he said. "I never thought I would be back so soon."

The anguish was palpable. I don't remember much of the rest of this visit, but I do remember them telling us that Priscilla needed to go to Sanford Hospital in Grand Forks because they had better technology there. They transported her there via ambulance, and we went back home and got the dog. I grabbed my computer because I felt like I might need it, and we rushed to Grand Forks, although there is no good way to rush there because it's sixty miles away.

We got to the hospital and they informed us that there was blood on her brain—a lot of blood, causing another stroke. I think they believed there wasn't much hope, but we thought to ourselves, "Well, we've done a stroke recovery before. She's just going to be different this time."

The neurologist, Kim, tried to explain to Priscilla's parents how the brain worked in her particular situation. When I said that I had a background in neuroscience, she seemed relieved, or at least comforted, by the fact that I might be able to help explain things. She showed them the CT scan taken of the brain and where it was filling up with blood.

"This is very, very serious, and your daughter is the sickest patient in this hospital right now," she said. "The only thing we might be able to do is to get her on a helicopter to Fargo where they can try and put coils in to take out some of the fluid."

Kim had told me that they needed to do a ventriculostomy tube, which was a tube placed inside the skull to drain the fluid. They shaved part of her head to prepare her and took her into surgery. The operation was successful. They could see the line from the tube to where the bag was filling up with fluid. I thought that was a good sign. She was reflexive, meaning that if you touched part of her, she would move a little bit. I think it was both a reaction to touch and her reflexes.

I don't remember much about the ride to Fargo except wondering when the helicopter had taken off. We never saw it leave the pad, but they arrived before we did. We were led past the waiting room; you know it's bad when they lead you to your own back room. It was a place that's no bigger than two shower stalls put together. It had two chairs and just enough room to sleep on the floor.

Two doctors came in. They informed us, in no uncertain terms, "Once there has been enough blood on the brain, the brain does not have anywhere else to put it. Blood is an irritant for the brain and basically kills it. This is what is known as brain death. I'm sorry to tell you that Priscilla has reached this point. There is nothing we can do but make her comfortable. It was at 11:15 p.m. that we made the determination."

I started crying and screamed, "No!" I knew the answer to the following question, but to try to give myself some sort of peace of mind, I asked it anyway. "So, if you take out the breathing tube, that's the end, right?"

"I'm afraid so, yes."

We all sat there in silence. That could not have been happening. Darlene requested that they call the rest of the family before taking her off life support. This was granted, and the doctors left the room.

And I screamed.

It was the high-pitched scream of somebody who was not in my body. Cledith and Darlene ran to the door to make sure that nobody had heard that awful noise or to escape that little room. I did it again because it was the only thing I knew how to do right then. Sometimes, noises speak louder than words.

I went into her room and sat down on the chair at her bedside. There she was, my little angel. Except this time, she looked like a little angel from some sort of cyborg movie. They had put a catheter in and an arterial line. I didn't dare touch anything for fear of knocking out the breathing tube or other tubes leading to who-knew-where. She was lying under a gown under a sheet. She was ice cold. There may as well have been frost on her fingers and toes. I held her hand and it was not clenched, but I would have preferred it to have been clinched because then I knew she still had strength. The breathing machine was so rhythmic that after a while, I began to make music with it. Tapping out certain rhythms depending on the inhale or the exhale.

I spoke to her, knowing that she couldn't hear me. I sang to her, although what song it was, I can't remember. I asked her to say hi to some friends we knew who had passed away in recent years.

I held her feet for an hour. The feet that had worn my favorite shoes many times. The feet that I had massaged thousands upon thousands of times. The feet that were often cold, but I could always warm up. I held her toes, but they never got warmer. They had evidently done a blood gas draw because there was tape by her heel.

Darlene came in and felt what I did, and we both looked at her in silence. This was not happening. Where was the smile? Where was the laughter? It was all replaced by a mechanical device performing a normally human function.

Priscilla's brother Dion and his family came down from Park River, arriving at about four in the morning. I went back to the little back room and slept for a bit because I had been up the whole time.

I don't recall what time I woke up. I felt like I was in some sort of crazy dream that I wished could end, so we could go back to the life we had created for ourselves. But I knew I needed to tell people what had happened. It was the part that I hated to do the most because of the nature in which I had to do it. I had to write a Facebook post. Social media was not the way I wanted to relay the news, but it was the only way to reach the thousands of people who loved Priscilla, including some I loved dearly myself.

The reality was slowly setting in that I was going to be alone with just Katie as my companion. I thought about how I had been alone before, but how different my life was going to be this time.

I don't recall much of the rest of the day except that they ran one more test, and we got lunch before we had to make the decision that we all knew was coming. The test was a blood dye test to check for brain activity. They wheeled her away, the ventriculostomy tube still in her skull, and her mouth covered by the breathing tube that was keeping her alive.

Darlene said, "I just want to make sure before we decide … just in case …"

Cledith and Trent didn't eat anything, but the rest of us had lunch. I was receiving tons of texts and a few phone calls. I used both of our phones and was alternately plugging them in to keep them charged.

We all knew in our hearts the test would come back negative. The dye ran throughout her bloodstream and stopped at the base of the skull. She was a shell. As I had told my parents through tears the night before, I lost my angel. There was only one thing left to do now. It was something I never thought I would do in my life, let alone at age thirty.

We all gathered around her bed, except Trent. I don't

think he ever went and saw her because he just couldn't. I don't blame him.

The chaplain came in, and I said, "I'm betting you have to do a lot of these."

His response was, "More than I would like to."

We all gazed upon Priscilla, the wife, daughter, sister, sister-in-law, aunt, and woman who had been so powerful in her own small way. She had never let anything stop her from accomplishing whatever mission she had set out to do. And then, there she was, attached to who-knows-how-many tubes and machines. Her power was gone. Her eyes were blank; her mouth wasn't talking. All that remained was the rhythmic sound of the breathing machine as we looked down upon her. I might've been the first one to say it.

"Well, it's time."

Nobody wanted to do it, of course. But I know for certain, and I might've said this at the time, that Priscilla Carlson NEVER wanted to be on life support. We had had this discussion just months before.

The chaplain said a prayer of some sort. The nurses came in, and I moved to the other side of her bed. They began unhooking her from the machines and tubes. Most of the family left the room except for Darlene, Dion, and me.

"There might be some blood when we take the breathing tube out, just to warn you." The nurse had been describing what they were doing, so I had the benefit of knowing. There was no blood. The tube was dry, which meant that there had been no brain activity for a while.

The breathing machine stopped. All that was left was her heartbeat. The family came in once again, and the torrents of tears became floods. We all put our hands on her chest, and they turned off the monitor. It's not like in the movies, in which the monitor is left on until it goes flat. Her heart sped up and seemed to be beating as fast as it always had. They said this would happen. I stepped back to let her family feel. Then I put my hand on her chest one more time and felt the heart slow down. The chest contracted in cardiac arrest, as if she were gasping for breath, but I knew there was no breath to be gasped. I let her parents feel her last heartbeats. It only seemed fitting as they had brought her into the world, that they should feel her last moments. The heart beat slower … slower … and then, at 2:02 p.m., Priscilla Carlson was gone.

CHAPTER SIXTEEN

An Angel at Peace

If you had told me on May 19, 2017, that one week later, I would be planning my wife's funeral, I would've told you to fuck off and that you were crazy. Exactly one week before, we had been closing up the office of Priscilla's recent job, and she was in considerable pain thanks to the ever-present kidney stone. That next day, we went to my parents' place to see my grandparents and celebrate my grandmother's eighty-ninth birthday. Priscilla took painkillers and tried to hide her pain when she got a cramp from the kidney stones. She was quiet at times, and I knew that's when the cramps were happening.

Priscilla tried to be as jovial as ever, but it was a bittersweet experience to see my grandmother. She was rapidly losing her short-term memory, so our conversations were looping and repetitive. For example, she didn't remember that it was her birthday or how old she was.

We tried to make light of the situation as much as possible. Priscilla and I gave her gift cards to Einstein Bros. Bagels, but handed them to my grandpa, who would remember what they were for. I kept reminding my grandmother through her ever-amplified hearing aids that we had gotten her those gift cards. That was the last time my parents, grandparents, and siblings saw Priscilla alive.

There I was, a week later, in a funeral home, the same funeral home where we had the memorial for Shane, Priscilla's cousin, nearly three years prior. The funeral director, Kim, made the process as painless as it could be. I can't really recall the specifics of the proceedings. I do know that there was a discussion about the flowers, and I immediately interjected that there should be as few roses and carnations as possible. Priscilla HATED those flowers because they smelled like … a funeral home. I think we did okay on that front.

We left Priscilla's spot at the kitchen table the way it was for a day or so, with her half-filled mug of coffee. Her green wheelchair remained in the spot where it had been when we took it out of the car before heading to Grand Forks. It is still in that same spot to this day. Sitting there, empty, the symbol of power and grace.

The people began showing up, and I don't

remember much of the weekend, except that I wrote several Facebook statuses and tried to organize my mind around what happened and how to proceed in my life. Funeral arrangements were still being made with the priest and Kim. Kim said that she embalmed Priscilla herself and that they would need a smaller casket, but not a child's casket, because Priscilla's body was too wide. They found one that was gold on the outside and white on the inside. It was 5'6" long as opposed to the usual 7' long casket, which would have made Priscilla look like a speck. They were driving it down from Minneapolis.

Doug and Sharon, Priscilla's uncle and aunt, came down on Sunday and stayed with us. We all sat around the table and reminisced. My family, Michelle, and Matt and the kids, and Teresa, Lisa, and Diane all showed up on Monday. My family had never been to Park River and weren't exactly sure what to make of it. Then we all had dinner.

I don't know which Priscilla hated more, carnations, or the idea of an after-funeral luncheon. I remember her saying, "It's fucking disgusting! Somebody dies, you bury them, and then you go and eat? That's a stupid tradition!"

Unfortunately, there was nothing we could do about that "stupid tradition" because if we didn't do it, then we looked cheap in the eyes of a town of about 1,200. So, it was either barbecue sandwiches or ham sandwiches, and lemon bars. We picked the latter because, as Darlene asked, "Who would want sloppy Joes at a funeral where everybody is dressed up?" I protested vehemently to having the lunch at all, but that's just what you do in a small town, so I had to suck it up. The women were nice enough to prepare something; so I gave in but did wonder what the expression on Priscilla's face would be after tasting the food.

Priscilla's Aunt Echo and I went through the music together. She was a singer in the church choir and knew a lot of the hymns and songs that I, being Jewish, hadn't a clue about. I wanted to pick the most positive, uplifting songs in that book of a thousand. Priscilla Carlson, if she could have had her ideal funeral, would have had a party complete with Bon Jovi's music blasting throughout the room. I did mention that to the priest who, unsurprisingly, was not too thrilled with the suggestion. Then I thought about how we could make *Livin' on a Prayer* into a gospel-inspired song. I didn't bring that part up to the priest, though.

The priest was a quirky guy with kind of a high, squeaky voice who always sounded as if the next word was the first time he had uttered whatever was about to come out of his mouth; a sort of inflection of surprise always seemed to be working around the next syllabic corner. I had no clue what he looked like, so I'm not sure if the voice and appearance matched.

Anyway, we wanted to see how this priest preached to get a sense of his style and how he would present the funeral. We didn't really have a choice of priest at such short notice, but it was a way to get a feel for him. That day was Trent's graduation day, and all of the Catholic kids were going to be at the Catholic church. There were six of them, including Trent.

I don't remember much about the priest's sermon because I was imagining how Priscilla used to read in that very church. She had had the clear, concise voice of somebody who was confident in what she was saying. Also, we were distracted by people giving us their sympathies. I do remember when the priest asked the kids, who were all up in the front row, "What do you need when you go to college next year?"

The answers varied.

"Your faith."

"A Bible."

"Textbooks."

To all of these, the priest responded, "NO!"

Had I been asked, my response would have been, "Easy Mac, a microwave, and toilet paper." But nobody asked me.

Finally, the priest exclaimed, "You need an alarm clock!"

I think everyone else in the congregation looked at each other as if to say, "Yeah, I'm not the only one who didn't think about that, right?"

Realizing there might be kids in front of him who might not know what an alarm clock was, he added,

"Although I guess I should bring myself into the times and say, 'You need your cell phone!'"

There was marked recognition amongst the six freshly tasseled youth. I knew Priscilla would approve of this character—someone who had studied enough to know the priesthood but was still laid back enough to make things interesting for his parishioners.

The day before the funeral, we went to see Priscilla in Grafton. We brought the clothes that she was to be dressed in. I had asked Kim if we could put shoes on her. She said that we could, but that nobody would see her feet. I explained that even though she couldn't walk, Priscilla was all about the shoes. I left out the fact that I enjoyed any excuse to buy them for her.

We picked out a black and gold velvet top (velvet is my favorite material), black pants, and the black shoes with gold studs on them that she had bought specifically for me, so that I could feel the studs. I did not complain because they were one of the hottest pairs she owned. And that was saying something. That trip was not one we wanted to make, but we wanted to see what our angel would look like before she was shown.

I never thought that the first corpse I would touch would be my life partner.

The mortician let us into the funeral home and told us to wait. In about twenty minutes, he said Priscilla was ready. We walked upstairs. It was a house that had been converted into a funeral home, and I found it ironic that a person who had never walked up a set of stairs in her life had just been carried up a steep staircase.

We walked into the room and there, on a cart, sat the casket. We had looked at the coffin in a book the other day. It seemed eerily like shopping for the blinds that we had picked out nearly three years earlier. When we had picked out the coffin, I couldn't feel its texture or what it would look like. I could only listen as the colors were chosen.

I put my hands on the shiny metal of the outside and felt the handles which I knew would be lifted for the last time the next day. Trailing my hands up the cold surface, my fingers came in contact with what felt like a soft blanket. This was the white part of the inside of the casket. The gold, I was told, did not look like it was made of an inexpensive gold-plated material. In other words, it looked like a nice coffin and was quite sparkly.

My fingers found their way up the soft blanket to the top side of the casket and then went inside. The sides were steeper than I thought they would be, but the proportions were also different.

And there she was. All dressed up in the clothes that we had brought.

The velvet was so soft, and I had forgotten that she had that shirt. I couldn't tell the difference between her pants and her skin, it seemed. Then I noticed how different she looked to me from a tactile point of view.

Her parents were quietly standing by, holding back

tears. Their biggest comment was about how well they had done with her hair, despite the ventriculostomy tube that had been placed in her skull. I was not allowed to touch her hair for fear of ruining it, which was understandable. I felt and found her hand. It was curled in the shirt that we had picked out and covered up the bruises from the IVs that she had endured less than a week before. But her skin didn't feel like skin anymore. It felt like wax. Her face and lips felt swollen and grotesque to the touch. Whether they looked that way to the eye, I will never know.

Even if somebody were to describe it to me one hundred times, what they saw and what I pictured in my mind will still always be different. I reached down while keeping one hand on her face and found the shoes that I loved so much. Like her hands, her feet were swollen more so than I had ever seen them in life (and this included the times she broke her ankles). My instinct was to take off the shoe as I had done for her only a week ago and to rub her feet to give them more circulation. It was a fleeting memory of what used to be.

I didn't dare remove any clothing because they had just gotten her dressed for us. Besides, that high arch in her foot that I loved so would not look the same as I wanted it to look in my mind. I examined every inch of her that I could. Tears were a constant companion to my exploration. She was swollen, and her chest was malformed, most likely as a result of the CPR. But you would only have known that if you knew her body the way I did. I had had the luxury of being permitted to touch her softly with fine, detailed precision many times.

I don't remember what I said, don't remember what we talked about while gazing upon her. It was surreal. I thought that nobody should have to go through this with their beloved. I am grateful that I didn't have to do that the next day at the actual funeral because I would already know what she looked like.

I wanted to talk to her, like I had done in the hospital with the breathing machine as a rhythmic background. I wanted to sing as I had done five days earlier. But I couldn't; we were in a place of business and the morticians had things to do. There were several stretches of silence, during which we all gazed down on her. The smell of the embalming agents and flowers mixed together to create a pungent gut-wrenching odor that she would have detested.

There she lay, propped up slightly on a pillow, as if she could open those beautiful eyes and say, "Good morning, I love you," as she had done thousands of days in a row. But that day she was a sleeping little angel.

We met with the priest for one last discussion of the readings that we had picked out. The rest of the day was a blur. I decided to keep her wedding ring, and I held it in between my thumb and forefinger while I sang "Rise Up" at the funeral. I didn't do that badly, but I didn't do that well, either.

Katie was very, very anxious, so much so that Dad

had to take her outside. You can embalm someone and cover them in flowers and makeup, but a dog knows who a person is. That was tough.

I remember people greeting me and the sound of the casket being rolled in. I remember not hearing them close the lid. I remember the readings, Shantel's voice cracking as she read the Bible verses, and the passion that went into the singing of the hymns. At the cemetery, the glittering casket was lowered into a vault that was just as sparkling. As I laid my hand on the gold lid for the last time, I knew that there was a golden angel above who could now be at peace.

A few weeks later, at the Celebration of Life that we held for Priscilla in Colorado, the following quote was placed at the head of her program. It was a comment in one of the Phamaly plays she was in, and sums up, I think, her outlook on the great beyond as only Priscilla could say it.

"Man, if I get to heaven and I'm still in a wheelchair, I'm going to be really pissed off!"

In 2015 and 2016, I took courses at the Coaches Training Institute (CTI). It is generically what is called Life Coaching (a term I dislike for various reasons), but it changed my life. I had always been a fan of the productivity method called Getting Things Done™ by David Allen. One of the coaches from this methodology recommended I check out CTI. Priscilla was able to take the five courses with me because I needed somebody to be my reader. One of the leaders of the courses, Rick Tamlyn, immediately saw the dynamic between the two of us as well as the ever-present Katie. Those courses changed the way Priscilla and I interacted with each other and with other people. We developed a self-advocacy presentation that we were going to use as the foundation for a coaching practice.

Since Priscilla's death, coaching has maintained a central place in my life, and I am always looking for clients who want to be more aware of people with disabilities or who have disabilities and want to be self-advocates. But I don't want it to stop with just one-on-one coaching sessions. I created the business In-Sightful Living as a platform for both coaching and keynote speaking. Priscilla's passion was social justice. My passions involve accessible technologies for the blind, the aforementioned coaching, and using my sense of humor and stories from this book to make people more aware of just how important being a self-advocate is for somebody with a disability.

I love being in front of an audience and have been told that I should go into standup comedy. At the end of the day, though, I want to speak to audiences and make them think, "Huh! I never thought about that before!" I don't want people to go away thinking, "Wow, that's so … inspirational," and then go back to life as usual. I want people to go away from my speeches thinking, "Damn, those two sure did a hell of a lot during their time together; seems like nothing stopped them. That's so cool!"

This book started out as a way to encapsulate all of the feelings that I had after Priscilla's death. It was the same kind of catharsis I had had after the conclusion of the Self-Advocacy Summit, and a way for me to honor her legacy and all that she fought for on a daily basis.

As I wrote, I realized that the overarching theme of the book was not just self-advocacy for people with disabilities, but also self-advocacy for people in relationships. It became apparent that one of the main facets of any relationship is communication. There are a surprising number of relationships (not just romantic) which suffer greatly from a lack of communication. The relationship that Priscilla and I had necessitated communication and became nearly telepathic. We had our own language and knew each other's physical actions and thoughts often before they were executed. This type of communication is rare, and we never took it for granted.

In the days after Priscilla's death, I began to sort through the tumult of emotions that were slamming into me. She had taught me to think more positively about life and not take it for granted as much as I had in the past. Unfortunately, for both of us, we learned that the hard way because several of our friends had passed away unexpectedly. Every time one did, we looked at each other and realized just how lucky we were.

Now that she was gone, I had to think about finding the positive in a dreadful and sad situation. The two main positives were that she was not in physical pain anymore and that I felt I had said everything I could say to her in the time we had together. Due to the strong bond that we had and our pledge to be open about our feelings toward each other, we told each other every day through words and actions how much our love meant to the other.

Priscilla always wanted to live a life without regrets. When she died, there were no arguments over something petty between us nor a disagreement that was lingering and needed to be resolved. We knew that her health was failing, but we didn't know just how much (at least I didn't know how much; what she knew will always remain a mystery.) Somehow, through the pain and anguish of losing her, I came to the conclusion that we were safe in the knowledge that we had lived the fullest life we could in the time that we had.

We did this through advocating for what we needed, whether from each other or from society, which required both vulnerability and communication. And if you take nothing else from this book, please hear this:

Without clear, concise communication, there is no self-advocacy.

Obituary

Priscilla Carlson (Feb. 20, 1978–May 25, 2017), 39 of Louisville, Colorado, formerly of Park River, North Dakota, passed away of a brain aneurysm, peacefully on Thursday, May 25, surrounded by family. Born with a brittle bone disorder known as osteogenesis imperfecta (OI), Priscilla was home schooled until age 12 when the Americans with Disabilities Act was passed. She graduated from Park River High School in 1995. After graduation, she worked in telemarketing and customer service, eventually becoming assistant sight supervisor and lead trainer. After meeting another individual with OI from Colorado, Priscilla moved there to take advantage of the accessibility of the Denver Metro area. She attended college at Front Range Community College and the University of Colorado Boulder where she graduated with a B.A. in Broadcast News Journalism and a B.S. in political science.

She met her husband in 2011, a year in which she suffered a serious fall from her power wheelchair, breaking eight bones in her legs, and then suffering a massive stroke on her left side. After re-learning how to speak, read, and write, she finished the two bachelor's degrees in December 2012.

She and David were married on June 27, 2014. Prior to her passing, she held a job at the JFK Partners Institute at the University of Colorado Boulder Anschutz Medical campus and as an associate at Walgreens.

Priscilla was a tireless advocate for those with and without disabilities. Social justice and fair treatment of minorities were hallmarks of her personality, along with a boundless sense of optimism. This was counterbalanced with an acerbic and quick wit, hampered only slightly by aphasia and disfluency after her stroke.

She will be missed by hundreds if not thousands of individuals.

An angel is with the angels. Rest in peace, Priscilla Darlene Carlson.

This is what I wrote on Facebook on the day of Priscilla's funeral.

Today we lay my angel, my soulmate, my love, to rest. A rest that means no pain, no kidney stones, no headaches. I hope, with my heart and soul, that eternity finally makes your bones strong, your feet and legs will walk, run, and jump, and your mind will be full of the love you gave to all of us on earth. May your spirit soar as your light shines over us all. Farewell my angel, my soulmate, my love.

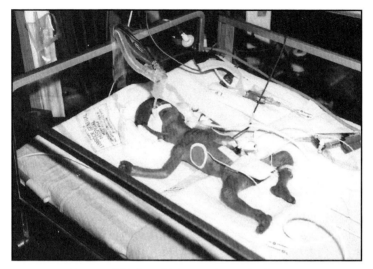

Dave at eight days old, born at 1 pound, 14 ounces

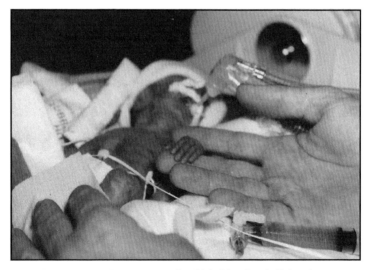

Dave at approximate two weeks old, holding his dad's hand

Dave as a toddler, playing with his toys

Dave as a young boy, learning to shave. Had he known how fast his facial hair would grow, he would have started shaving a lot earlier!

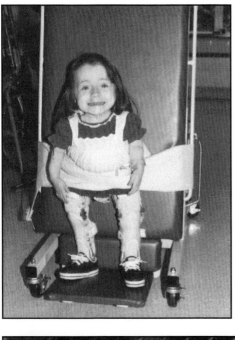

Priscilla at age five, smiling while wearing leg braces and strapped to an upright board to emulate a standing position.

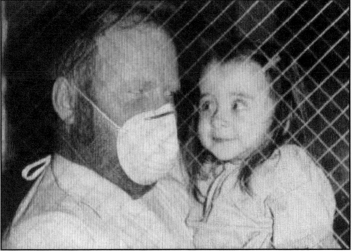

Priscilla at age five with her father, Cledith, holding her in his arms in the isolation chamber during her five-month stay in the hospital to cure a staph infection. The expression on Priscilla's face seems to say, "Okay Dad, we gonna make a break for it?"

Dave with famed blind author and motivational speaker
Tom Sullivan in March 2002.

Dave and Priscilla celebrate her graduation from
CU Boulder, December 2012.

Dave graduates from CU
Boulder with a Masters in
Musicology, May 2013.

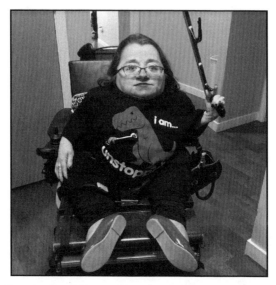

Priscilla wears her Halloween costume consisting t-shirt with a T-Rex holding a reacher and the word "unstoppable" and Priscilla holding a reacher just like the T-Rex

Katie the Guide Dog holding a "toothbrush" chew toy and the angle of the toy makes it look like she's smoking a cigar.

Priscilla looks over her shoulder while piloting her beloved car, the Enterprise. Note the cool gadgets and dash controls designed specifically for Priscilla

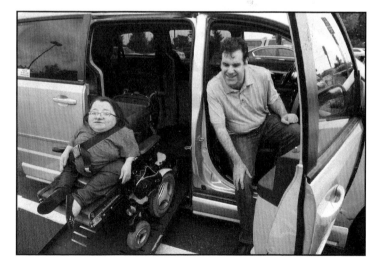

Dave and Priscilla exit the Enterprise, Dave from the passenger's seat and Priscilla from the ramp that comes out the side sliding door. Team Prave off on another adventure!

Dave, Priscilla, and Katie the Guide Dog pose for an engagement picture on the CU Boulder campus in 2014.

Dave and Priscilla pose with their engagement rings in 2014.

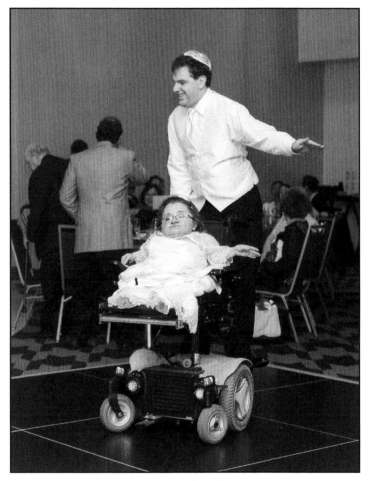

Dave rides on the back of Priscilla's wheelchair as they make their entrance for their wedding dance on June 27, 2014.

ACKNOWLEDGMENTS

It would behoove me in the interests of recognition to place two pairs of individuals at the top of the list of the following to whom this book is indebted. I must thank both my parents, Chuck and Michele, and Priscilla's parents, Cledith and Darlene. If it weren't for them, none of this would've happened.

If the saying, "It takes a village" is true for any sort of production, I did not realize just how big of a village it would take to produce the *Prave* book. I must thank my writing coach/consultant/sounding board Kris Jordan for patiently waiting for drafts to come through and sometimes literally yelling at me to get the words out onto the page when it was the most difficult. Thank you to my editor, Catherine Spader, for doing a fantastic job of tightening up the prose while still keeping my voice and wit intact. Thank you to Nick Zelinger at NZ Graphics for the amazing cover and working through all of the different revisions. Nick is also to be singled out here for trying to explain things like colors, shadings, and fonts to a blind person in a way that I could understand.

Finally, thank you to the staff at My Word Publishing for giving guidance on who to talk to about editing, cover design, and proofreading.

In a non-professional role, I'd like to thank all of the people who heard about the book as I was going along and encouraged me to keep writing it. Special thanks go to Jon Fisher and Michelle Hawkins for their unwavering commitment to *Prave* as a couple and as a concept. I must also thank Mr. Rick Tamlyn for having a dream of *Prave* when he first set eyes on us at the Coaches Training Institute class. He has continued to champion me through the toughest of times.

If I have missed anyone specifically in the above acknowledgments, please wave at me the next time you see me, or point, I'm sure that'll get my attention. If I didn't acknowledge you, and you happen to be blind, well, I guess you'll never get that acknowledgment since we can't see each other as we pass by!

No, in all seriousness, those who I have not had the space to mention here know who you are and are thanked from the bottom of my heart for making this book go from a cathartic overture into the multi-movement symphonic portrait that it has become.

ABOUT THE AUTHOR

Having a vision does not require sight, just insight.

Dave Bahr is an author, speaker, and comedian focused on demystifying the public's perception of how to interact with people with disabilities. As founder of In-Sightful Living, Dave works as an accessibility consultant, aiding organizations to enhance their systems, environments, events, and cultures to be supportive of people with disabilities. Blind from birth, he teaches that having a disability is not a hindrance, but an asset.

Dave holds a B.A. in Psychology and a Masters of Historical Musicology from the University of Colorado at Boulder and is proud to have studied with the Coaches Training Institute to further his personal development and leadership skills.

Dave's funny and often irreverent wit allows him to use storytelling to illustrate that people should not be afraid of disability. He encourages curiosity, tact, and humor over political correctness, fear, and ignorance.

Dave can be reached via In-SightfulLiving.com.